Key Stage 3
Science Lab Book

Get ready for GCSE (9–1)

Ed Walsh

William Collins' dream of knowledge for all began with the publication of his first book in 1819.
A self-educated mill worker, he not only enriched millions of lives, but also founded a flourishing publishing house. Today, staying true to this spirit, Collins books are packed with inspiration, innovation and practical expertise. They place you at the centre of a world of possibility and give you exactly what you need to explore it.

Collins. Freedom to teach.

Published by Collins
An imprint of HarperCollins*Publishers*
The News Building
1 London Bridge Street, London, SE1 9GF

HarperCollins*Publishers*
Macken House, 39/40 Mayor Street Upper,
Dublin 1, D01 C9W8, Ireland

Browse the complete Collins catalogue at
www.collins.co.uk

10 9 8

ISBN 978-0-00-834247-0

British Library Cataloguing-in-Publication Data
A catalogue record for this publication is available from the British Library.

Author: Ed Walsh
Commissioning editor: Katie Sergeant
In-house editor: Joanna Ramsay
Development editor: Joanne Crosby
Copyeditor and designer: Anna Clark
Proofreader and answer checkers: Joan Miller, Aidan Gill
Artwork: Jouve
Cover designer: Julie Martin
Cover photo: Anest/Shutterstock
Production controller: Katharine Willard
Printed and bound in India by Replika Press Pvt. Ltd.

This book contains FSC™ certified paper and other controlled sources to ensure responsible forest management.

For more information visit: www.harpercollins.co.uk/green

The publishers gratefully acknowledge the permission granted to reproduce the copyright material in this book. Every effort has been made to trace copyright holders and to obtain their permission for the use of copyright material. The publishers will gladly receive any information enabling them to rectify any error or omission at the first opportunity. *We are grateful to the following for permission to reproduce copyright material:*
Page 30, bottom right, Richard Griffin/Shutterstock

Contents

Schools can download mapping to GCSE (9–1), answers and record sheets at www.collins.co.uk.

How to use this book

Practical work is a really important part of science. There are three good reasons why doing experiments is part of your science education.

- The first is that it's a good way of learning how to use equipment. Using a microscope, being able to weigh accurately and knowing how to set up a circuit are just a few of the skills you should develop whilst studying science.
- Second, it's important that you know how to investigate scientifically. Using evidence to write a conclusion, for example, is an important skill. Seeing if a new design of car meets safety standards for example or analysing archaeological remains to suggest how an ancient civilisation lived are only possible if this has been mastered.
- Third, it can be a good way of understanding ideas. Students often say that if they can see something happening it's a good way of understanding it.

This book includes a number of features that we think will be helpful. Some you may find more useful than others. The important thing is that you have a go. Scientists don't always get it right and experiments don't always work. That doesn't mean that nothing has been learned.

- **Mini vocabulary warm up.** Science has its own language and you need to be familiar with the words relevant to the investigation you are going to do. The words are important because they are rather like handles – they enable you to get hold of concepts. Some of these questions involve selecting the right word, some are true/false statements and some involve a group of students who you will keep meeting in different experiments. They have their own ideas and it's quite possible that you will agree with some of the things they say.
- **Details of the practical activity.** This includes the purpose of the experiment, how to set it up, the method you should follow and space to enter your results. We've suggested suitable equipment, identified some mistakes to avoid and also made some important points about safety. We not only want you to avoid accidents but also to learn how to make decisions about safe working.
- **Analyse results.** Having done the experiment, you need to make sense of what you've found out. Think of this as the 'so what?' stage – you've got the evidence and you now need to suggest what that shows. Be clear about what you've learned by doing the experiment.
- **Check your understanding.** By this stage you'll have done quite a lot since the start of the experiment so it's probably a good idea to revisit some of the key ideas.
- **Spot the mistake**. This is where you'll meet our friendly students again. As you'll see, they don't always get things right. An important skill is being able to suggest why.
- **Apply your understanding.** It's important to understand that often when you do an experiment the ideas can be applied to other situations as well. The questions in this section are to help you make those links.
- **Evaluate your learning.** Having done the experiment and answered some questions, you'll probably have quite a good idea of how well you did. Having a sense of what you did well and what you might focus on the next time you do an experiment is a key part of being a scientist.

You'll be aware that some time later in your education you'll be thinking about GCSE qualifications. That's in the future and will seem quite a long way off yet. Practical work is also an important part of GCSE Science courses though, and if you do these experiments and answer some of the questions it will make doing those experiments less of a big change.

Above all, don't worry. Do the experiments, have a go at the questions and see what you can learn. Remember, the scientific ideas we have came from people doing experiments and finding things out.

> *Teachers should always ensure they consult the latest CLEAPSS safety guidance before undertaking any practical work.*

Mini vocabulary warm up

Look at these words:

cell   membrane   slide   microscope   eyepiece   objective

Which of these: (Note: each word may be used more than once.)

1. is the rectangular piece of glass on which objects are placed for viewing under a microscope?

    .... [1 mark]

2. is a device used to magnify small objects? .... [1 mark]

3. refers to the lenses on the microscope? .... and .... [2 marks]

4. is the lens closest to the object? .... [1 mark]

5. is the lens closest to the eye? .... [1 mark]

6. is regarded as the 'building block' of all living things? .... [1 mark]

7. is a thin layer around the edge of a cell? .... [1 mark]

8. Zena's group are looking at an old oak tree and discussing the cells in it.

Zena: I think the leaves and the acorns are made of cells, but not the trunk and branches. They're too solid.	Will: I agree about the leaves and acorns, but I think there's softer material inside the trunk that's made of cells too.	Emile: I think it's all made of cells – even the really knarled bits on the outside.

   Who do you think is right and why?

   ....

   ....[2 marks]

9. Kursad's group are looking at objects through a microscope. On the side of the eyepiece lens, it says ×10 and on the side of the objective lens it says ×4. He puts his ruler under the microscope and looks at the 1 mm markings.

    a. How far apart will they appear? (circle the correct option)   [1 mark]

        1 mm   10 mm   14 mm   40 mm

    Kursad says, 'Actually, we should put a minus sign in front of the distance.'

    b. Why do you think he says that?

        .... [1 mark]

    c. Is he right? Give a reason for your answer.

        .... [1 mark]

Purpose of practical activity

In this activity you are going to be examining and recording cells in a plant. The plant you are going to analyse is a bell pepper. These are quite common and come in red, yellow or green varieties.

If you examine a bell pepper carefully, using a microscope, you should be able to see giant cells – these are larger than many of the other cells in a bell pepper and in many other plants. You should be able to identify, measure and draw these giant cells. There are also smaller cells, which you should be able to see too.

Learning outcomes	Maths skills required
• Use equipment to produce clear, focused images of microscopic objects. • Record images by drawing.	• Use of scale and proportion skills when magnifying.

Set up

Apparatus list
• ¼ of a red pepper per group   • Blunt forceps   • Cutting tiles   • Microscopes   • Scalpels   • Hand lenses   • Microscope slides and cover slips   • Mounted needles   • Paper towels

Safety notes
• *Tell your teacher if you have to avoid skin contact with bell peppers due to an allergy.*   • *Do not taste the pepper.*   • *Microscopes that use daylight illumination via a mirror must never be used where direct sunlight can strike the mirror, as serious eye damage will be caused.*   • *Take care when using sharp instruments such as scalpels, scissors and mounted needles, and follow any instructions for their safe use.*

Common mistakes and how to avoid them
• Make sure you place the piece of pepper the correct way up – the giant cells are visible on the inside.   • Make sure it is the pericarp and not the septum you are looking at.   • When you take sections of the pericarp, make sure you are getting a cross-section.

Method

Read these instructions carefully before you start work.

1. Using a cutting tile and a scalpel, carefully cut a piece of bell pepper pericarp 2 cm × 2 cm.

2. Using a hand lens, examine the inner surface of the pericarp. The long thin structures that you can see are giant cells.

3. Gently prod one of the giant cells with the point of a mounted needle and see how it feels.

4. Make a large, fully labelled drawing of a small number of the giant cells.

5. Look carefully, and you will see that the giant cells are covered by much smaller cells. These are called endocarp cells and are just visible through a hand lens.

6. Place the piece of pepper pericarp onto the cutting tile, with the giant cells uppermost. Cut a thin section of the pericarp (using a bread-slicing action) and mount it on a microscope slide in a drop of water, under a cover slip. Examine with an optical microscope and look for the pericarp and giant cells. Make a large, fully labelled drawing.

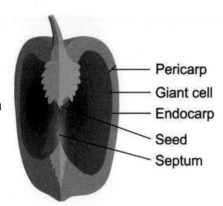

— Pericarp
— Giant cell
— Endocarp
— Seed
— Septum

Results

1. Use this box to record your drawing of the giant cells as seen through the hand lens.

2. Use this box to record your drawing of the endocarp and giant cells as seen through the microscope.

Analyse results

1. How would you describe the shape of one of the giant cells?

....

2. When you prodded the giant cell with a mounted needle, how did it feel?

....

Check your understanding

1. What structures divide one plant cell from another?

   ....[2 marks]

2. Some plant cells have chloroplasts – why don't the bell peppers you investigated have these?

   ....[2 marks]

3. What is the plant cell filled with? .... [1 mark]

Spot the mistake

1. Kareem's group opted not to bother with the hand lens and just used the microscope at the highest magnification to look for the giant cells. They could not get a clear focused image – why was this?

   ....[2 marks]

2. Amy looked at the cells through the microscope and then did a drawing that looked rather like bricks in a wall, with perfect rectangles. 'The cells must be like this,' she said, 'or they wouldn't fit together.' Why was this a mistake?

   ....[2 marks]

Apply your understanding

1. When you prodded one of the giant cells, you will have found that it is firm. Why is this important?

   ....[1 mark]

2. The pepper develops from the ovary of the fertilised flower. If you look inside a pepper, you will see the seeds. What purpose do you think the pepper serves?

   ....[2 marks]

Evaluate your learning

1. How well do you think you used the equipment to study the cells closely?

   ....

   ....

2. How well did you record the appearance of the cells by drawing them?

   ....

   ....

Mini vocabulary warm up

Look at these words:

exchange   gas   leaf   photosynthesis   carbon dioxide   water

Which of these:

1. refers to the gaseous reactant in photosynthesis? ....[1 mark]

2. is the liquid reactant in photosynthesis? .... [1 mark]

3. is the process by which plants produce glucose and oxygen? .... [1 mark]

4. is the part of the plant in which most of the photosynthesis takes place? .... [1 mark]

5. is a process in which one material is swapped for another? ....[1 mark]

6. is the state of matter in which volume is not fixed? .... [1 mark]

Each of the following statements is either **true** or **false** – choose the correct response.

7. Stomata are tiny openings that allow gas to enter or leave a plant. **True / False**   [1 mark]

8. Stomata open wider when the conditions are hot and dry. **True / False**   [1 mark]

9. Stomata allow carbon dioxide to enter a leaf. **True / False**   [1 mark]

10. Carbon dioxide is needed for respiration. **True / False**   [1 mark]

11. Zena's group are talking about plants and photosynthesis.

Zena: I'd never thought about plants breathing until now. I suppose they do though, don't they? They need to get gases in and out, just like we do.

Michelle: They don't breathe though. I mean, you don't see a plant with its leaves forcing air in and out.

Gina: Maybe it's something to do with size. We have to force air in and out because we're much bigger than a leaf. A leaf is smaller and it's really thin so the gases don't have to travel far to get in and out.

Read what the students are saying and think about their ideas. Is it correct to refer to leaves as breathing? Say what you think and explain why you think that.

....

....

....[3 marks]

Purpose of practical activity

In this activity you will examine stomata on leaves. Stomata (singular is stoma) are tiny openings in the leaf surface that open and close to allow intake of carbon dioxide and release of oxygen. Stomata can be studied by painting nail varnish onto the surface of a leaf and, when the nail varnish is dry, sticking adhesive tape onto it and peeling it off. The layer of varnish can be examined under a microscope − it will show details of the surface of the leaf.

You can use this technique to compare the upper and lower surfaces of the leaf. It should be possible to examine whether stomata tend to be on the top or bottom of a leaf.

Learning outcomes
• To use a procedure to give clear images to be analysed microscopically.   • To gather evidence to support a conclusion.   • To find out whether stomata are more likely to be found on the upper or lower surfaces of a leaf.

Set up

Apparatus list
• Leaves (Various types work well but the best results are generally achieved with ferns or leaves with a smooth surface.)   • Transparent adhesive tape   • Clear nail polish/varnish   • Microscopes   • Tweezers

Safety notes
• *Nail polish/varnish contains volatile solvents, which give off irritant vapours. Avoid inhaling the vapours and tell your teacher if it makes you feel unwell. Work in a well-ventilated area and not too close to others.*   • *Microscopes that use daylight illumination via a mirror must never be used where direct sunlight can strike the mirror as serious eye damage will be caused.*

Common mistakes and how to avoid them
• Make sure the nail varnish is dry before applying the tape.   • When you apply the tape, press down firmly to make sure the tape has stuck to the varnish. You can check by carefully peeling up one corner to see if the varnish lifts up too.   • Some leaves are quite large and it can be difficult to count all the stomata on the whole leaf. It is a good idea to work on the portion of the leaf that can be viewed through the microscope.

Method

Read these instructions carefully before you start work.

1.   Place the leaf flat on the bench, with the side that you want to examine facing up.

2.   Paint a thin layer of clear nail polish on the leaf.

3.   After a few minutes, carefully test a corner of the nail polish to make sure it is completely dry.

4.   Put a piece of tape over the nail polish on your leaf. Rub your finger over the tape to make sure it is stuck well to the nail polish. Note: sometimes the nail varnish can be peeled off easily with tweezers and tape is not needed.

5. Using tweezers, slowly peel the tape off the leaf. The nail polish should stick to the tape (not the leaf).

6. Stick the tape in the centre of a microscope slide. Then place the slide under your microscope.

7. Examine the image and draw what you see. Mark any shapes that you think could be stomata. Make sure you label the diagram, stating whether it is from the upper or lower side of the leaf.

Thin outer wall
Guard cells
Thick inner wall
Nucleus
Chloroplast

Stoma open   Stoma closed

8. Count the stomata you have found in this view.

9. Now repeat the procedure for the other side of the leaf.

Results

1. Do your first drawing in the box here.

Is this the upper or lower side? ………………………………

Number of stomata identified: ………………………………..

2. Do your second drawing in the box here.

Is this the upper or lower side? ………………………………

Number of stomata identified: ………………………………..

Analyse results

1. How well did the method of examining the leaf surface work?

   ....

   ....

2. What did you find out about the number of stomata on the upper side of the leaf compared with the lower side?

   ....

3. Suggest why you think this should be.

   ....

   ....

Check your understanding

1. What is the function of the stomata?

   ....

   ....[2 marks]

2. Under what conditions would you expect the stomata to be closed?

   .... [1 mark]

3. Why do you think this would be?

   .... [1 mark]

Spot the mistake

1. Zena's group could only see part of the leaf through the microscope and so moved the slide around to see (and count) all the stomata on each side. Why is this unlikely to give an accurate total number?

   ....

   ....[2 marks]

2. Gina's group realised that there was more than one type of leaf being studied and compared the number of stomata on the upper side of one type of leaf with the number on the lower side of a different type. Why was this a mistake?

   ....

   ....[2 marks]

Apply your understanding

1. Emile says, 'Stomata cells are a bit like gatekeepers aren't they?' Do you think he's right, and why?

   ....

   ....[2 marks]

2. Will's group are studying the stomata of plants grown in a greenhouse.

   Will: I think that we'll find more stomata on the upper side of a leaf than on the lower side. Stomata let in carbon dioxide for photosynthesis and that happens where it's light.

   Juanita: I think we'll find more stomata on the under side of the leaf. When it rains, ones on the upper side would let in water and the leaf would get waterlogged.

   Kareem: I think we'll find a similar number on both sides of the leaf. The leaf is made entirely of cells and they all need carbon dioxide.

   Explain who you think is right and why.

   ....

   ....[2 marks]

3. Suggest whether you would expect to find a similar distribution of stomata between the upper and lower surfaces of a leaf on a different type of plant. Explain your answer.

   ....

   ....

   ....[3 marks]

Evaluate your learning

1. In this experiment, you needed to create a clearly focused and well-prepared image of a leaf surface that you could then examine for stomata. How well do you think you did this?

   ....

   ....

   ....

2. The purpose of the experiment was to compare the distribution of stomata between the upper and lower surfaces of the leaf. How well do you think you managed to explore this?

   ....

   ....

   ....

Mini vocabulary warm up

Look at these words:

digestion   sugar   starch   carbohydrate   nutrition   bloodstream

Which of these:

1. is the process of breaking down foods to get the nutrients? .... [1 mark]

2. is the study of the effect of substances from food on the body? .... [1 mark]

3. is how nutrients are transported around the body? .... [1 mark]

4. is a foodstuff that provides you with energy quickly? .... [1 mark]

5. is a foodstuff that releases energy more slowly? .... [1 mark]

6. is a group of foodstuffs that includes sugar and starch? .... [1 mark]

Each of the following statements is either **true or false** – choose the correct response.

7. Digestion only happens in your stomach. **True / False**   [1 mark]

8. There are many different types of sugar. **True / False**   [1 mark]

9. Digestion has only one role – to get energy from food. **True / False**   [1 mark]

10. Potatoes and pasta contain starch. **True / False**   [1 mark]

11. Saliva helps to digest food. **True / False**   [1 mark]

12. Your body can get whatever it needs no matter what you eat. **True / False**   [1 mark]

13. Michelle is discussing with her friends what she eats for breakfast.

Michelle: My mum wants me to have porridge because she says it releases energy slowly to keep me going. I want to have Sugar Fluffs; they taste nicer and I need the energy straight away. I get energy from both of them so I don't think it matters whether it's released quickly or slowly.

Gina: Your mother thinks that slow release means you'll still be getting energy from your breakfast several hours later.

Zena: You get energy from both of them so they must have the same chemicals in them. Have the one you like!

Emile: I think there are other reasons for having porridge. The sugar in Sugar Fluffs isn't good for your teeth.

Write a brief response to each of the characters, saying what you think of each of their points.

a. Gina: .... [1 mark]

b. Emile: .... [1 mark]

c. Zena: .... [1 mark]

Purpose of practical activity

In this experiment you are going to test different types of foods to find out what they contain. There are many food types that can be tested for – in this activity you will be testing for starch and glucose. Both of these are found in a variety of foods.

Learning outcomes
<ul><li>Test foods for glucose and starch.</li><li>Analyse the results to see what is contained in a range of foods.</li><li>Draw conclusions about food nutrition.</li></ul>

Set up

Apparatus list
<ul><li>Variety of foods, chopped into small pieces – for example, crisps, bread, pasta, rice, chocolate, apple, banana, yoghurt, cheese</li><li>Test tubes</li><li>Benedict's solution</li><li>Iodine</li><li>Beakers</li></ul> <ul><li>Eye protection</li><li>Mortars and pestles</li><li>Heating equipment: if possible use a large water bath for the whole class, if this is not available use heatproof mats, tripods, gauzes, splints and Bunsen burners</li><li>Dimple tiles (if available)</li></ul>

Safety notes
<ul><li>*Wear eye protection during all practical activity and until everyone has finished clearing up.*</li><li>*Avoid skin contact with the Benedict's solution and only heat it with the food sample in a water bath or a beaker of hot water. Do not heat it directly over a flame.*</li><li>*Do not taste any of the food samples and wash your hands after you have finished handling them.*</li></ul>

Common mistakes and how to avoid them
<ul><li>You may have to grind up food samples before the glucose test can be used.</li><li>When using Benedict's solution, the contents of the test tube should be hot but not boiling. A good way of doing this is to use a beaker of water as a water bath for the test tubes to go in.</li><li>Make sure, if you are testing several different foodstuffs, that you do not cross-contaminate by getting bits of one sample in another, as this will affect the results.</li></ul>

Method

Read these instructions carefully before you start work.

Testing for starch

1. Place a sample of the food to be tested on a dimple tile (if one is available) and add a few drops of iodine. Avoid getting iodine on your fingers as it stains.

2. Watch to see what colour the sample goes. A blue-black colour indicates the presence of starch.

3. Record the food, the colour change and what this shows in the table.

Testing for glucose

1. Take a sample of the food to be tested and, if it is a solid lump, grind it up with a mortar and pestle.

2. Place the food sample in a test tube, add a few millilitres of water to the test tube and a few drops of Benedict's solution, then place the test tube in a beaker of hot water or a water bath for a few minutes. Watch to see what colour the mixture goes. A brick-red colour indicates the presence of glucose.

3. Record the food, the colour change and what this shows in the table.

Results

Food being tested	Colour after iodine is added	Results of test for starch (positive or negative)	Colour after being heated with Benedict's solution	Results of test for glucose (positive or negative)

Analyse results

1. a. List the foods that you found contained starch.

   ....

   b. List the foods that you found contained glucose.

   ....

   c. Do your results for the starch and glucose tests agree with those from other groups in the class?

   ....

2. Glucose is a sugar, so you would expect foods that test positive for glucose to taste sweet. (Note that tasting foods should not happen in a science lab).

   a. Looking at your results, is this true?

   ....

   b. Are there any foods which have a sweet taste that tested negative?

   ....

3. Foods that are widely known to contain starch include bread, rice and pasta. Look at the results for the starch test. Are there any surprises in your results?

....

....

Check your understanding

1. If you tested a food for glucose and ended up with a blue solution after you'd heated it for a few minutes, what would this show?

.... [1 mark]

2. If you tested a food for starch and ended up with a reddish brown colour on the food, what would this show?

.... [1 mark]

Spot the mistake

1. Juanita's group tested several different foods, including cracker biscuits, cheese, chocolate biscuits, shortbread and lettuce. They all tested positive for glucose. What might the group have done wrong?

....

.... [1 mark]

2. Will's group tested a piece of bread for both starch and glucose. They did the starch test first and put iodine on the bread. They then put that piece of bread in the mortar and pestle and ground it up to go in water and Benedict's solution. Why was this a mistake?

....

.... [1 mark]

Apply your understanding

1. Gina knows that glucose is not the only type of sugar and she also knows that the Benedict's solution test only works with glucose. She suggests, therefore, that some sweet foods would test negative for glucose and another sugar could be making them sweet. What do you think?

....

.... [1 mark]

17

2. In Science, Kareem's group have been learning about carbohydrates. The teacher has explained that starch gets broken down into glucose so it can be absorbed by the body.

Emile: There's no point in eating starchy foods – it all gets turned into glucose anyway. We might as well just eat sweet foods and save the body the trouble.

Zena: When I'm ill my Dad gives me a glucose drink. That must be so my body can get energy quickly to help it recover.

Kareem: I need loads of energy to do 100 m and 200 m sprints. Eating a bag of chips just before a race should help. My body will convert the starch in the chips into glucose to give me extra energy.

Comment on each of these ideas, explaining your reasoning.

a. Emile: ....

.... [1 mark]

b. Zena: ....

.... [1 mark]

c. Kareem: ....

.... [1 mark]

Evaluate your learning

1. In this experiment, you had to run a series of tests and gather evidence to complete a table. How well do you think you did this?

   ....

   ....

   ....

2. You had to work carefully to ensure that food from one test did not contaminate the food from another. How do you know how successful you were in preventing contamination from affecting your results?

   ....

   ....

   ....

Mini vocabulary warm up

Look at these words: **oxygen**   **chlorophyll**   **carbon dioxide**   **light**   **glucose**   **water**

Which of these:

1. is a gas and a product in photosynthesis? .... [1 mark]

2. is a gas and a reactant in photosynthesis? .... [1 mark]

3. must be present, in addition to the reactants, for photosynthesis to take place? (Give **two** words.)

    ....[2 marks]

4. is a liquid and a reactant in photosynthesis? .... [1 mark]

5. is a product of photosynthesis and provides the plant with energy? .... [1 mark]

Each of the following statements is either **true** or **false** – choose the correct response.

6. Photosynthesis happens when it's light and respiration happens when it's dark.
    True / False   [1 mark]

7. Respiration needs sunlight to happen. **True / False**   [1 mark]

8. Photosynthesis is a chemical reaction. **True / False**   [1 mark]

9. Plants respire continuously. **True / False**   [1 mark]

10. Photosynthesis cannot happen under water. **True / False**   [1 mark]

11. Kursad's group have been learning about photosynthesis

Kursad: Photosynthesis is the opposite of respiration. Respiration means taking in oxygen and releasing carbon dioxide, but photosynthesis means taking in carbon dioxide and releasing oxygen.

Gina: Photosynthesis is nothing like respiration. Photosynthesis needs chlorophyll and light; they've got nothing to do with respiration.

Will: I think it's about energy. When plants photosynthesise, they trap energy from the Sun in glucose, whereas respiration releases energy.

Comment on each of those ideas, clearly indicating what you think.

Kursad: ....

....

Gina: ....

....

Will:..

....[3 marks]

Purpose of practical activity

In this experiment you will be investigating the effect of the absence of light on photosynthesis. We know from the word equation for photosynthesis that light is necessary; the function of this experiment is to prove this. We will do this by stopping light from falling on part of a leaf and then testing the whole leaf to see if starch is present throughout, using iodine as the indicator. If there is no starch in the areas that had no light falling on them, this will indicate that light is necessary.

Learning outcomes

- Demonstrate that light is necessary for photosynthesis.
- Follow a sequence of instructions to produce evidence.
- Analyse evidence to support a conclusion.

Set up

Apparatus list

- Potted plants
- Black paper
- Paper clips
- Scissors
- Rulers/tape measures
- White tiles
- Iodine
- Beakers (250 ml)
- Eye protection
- Bunsen burners
- Forceps
- Boiling tubes
- Ethanol
- Water

Safety notes

- *Always be careful when handling chemicals and follow your teacher's safety advice about ethanol (see CLEAPSS guidance).*
- *Wear eye protection when boiling the leaf and when using ethanol.*
- *Ethanol is highly flammable and must never be heated with a Bunsen burner. Before the ethanol is opened every Bunsen burner must be turned off and not lit again until the ethanol is removed from the laboratory.*
- *The laboratory should be well ventilated if lots of students are using beakers of ethanol.*

Common mistakes and how to avoid them

- Plant not being destarched beforehand.
- Black paper being too small or loosely attached.
- Leaf not being boiled for long enough.

Method

Read these instructions carefully before you start work.

1. The plant needs to have been destarched beforehand by being kept in a dark place for 2–3 days.

2. Take a piece of black paper about 2 cm wide. It needs to be long enough to go round the front and back of the leaf, so that a broad strip is covered. A good starting point is to measure the width of the leaf, double it and add 1 cm.

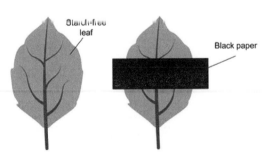

Starch-free leaf

Black paper

3. Fold the strip around one of the leaves on the plant and attach it by means of a paper clip (note: do not detach the leaf from the plant). The strip should prevent light from reaching part of the leaf so it needs to fit snugly. However, it is important to avoid damaging the leaf and it is also important to make sure there is also another part of the leaf that light does get to.

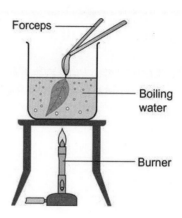
Forceps

Boiling water

Burner

4. Leave the plant in bright sunshine for several hours.

5. Set up a beaker two-thirds full of water and heat until boiling.

6. Detach the leaf from the plant and remove the black paper. Immerse the leaf in the boiling water for 10 minutes. Use forceps to hold it and ensure that it does not float on the surface

7. Turn out the Bunsen burner; it is essential to check there are no naked flames in the room before proceeding to the next stage.

8. Put the leaf into a boiling tube about half-full of ethanol and place the boiling tube in the beaker of hot water for 10 minutes.

9. Now use the forceps to remove the leaf; spread it out carefully on the white tile.

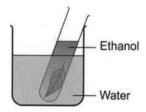
Ethanol

Water

10. Add drops of iodine to the surface of the leaf and watch to see where it goes blue-black, indicating the presence of starch.

Results

Draw the outline of the leaf and shade in on your drawing the areas where the iodine went blue-black.

Analyse results

1. Look at the leaf. What was the relationship between the covered and uncovered areas of the leaf and where starch was detected?

   ....

   ....

2. What conclusion can you draw from this?

   ....

   ....

Check your understanding

1. Compare the leaf before and after it was put in the boiling water. Why was placing the leaf in boiling water an important part of the process?

   .... [1 mark]

2. Compare the ethanol before and after the leaf was in it. Why did it change in appearance?

   .... [1 mark]

3. Why was it essential to check there were no naked flames before the ethanol was used?

   .... [1 mark]

4. Why did the ethanol boil, even though the Bunsen flame was out and the water had dropped below boiling point?

   .... [1 mark]

5. In this experiment:

   a. what was the independent variable? .... [1 mark]

   b. what was the dependent variable? .... [1 mark]

   c. what were the control variables? .... [1 mark]

Spot the mistake

1. Zena's group decided that there was no need to boil the leaf in water, so they skipped that stage and put the plucked leaf straight into the ethanol. Why was this a mistake?

   ....

   ....[2 marks]

2. Emile's group could not find any starch in their green leaf. What might they have done wrong?

....

....[2 marks]

3. Michelle's group found starch throughout their green leaf. What might they have done wrong?

....

....[2 marks]

Apply your understanding

1. The plant was destarched by leaving it in the dark for two or three days. Where do you think the starch went?

....

....[2 marks]

2. The process of photosynthesis produces glucose, not starch. What do you think the plant does with the glucose it has made?

....

....[2 marks]

Evaluate your learning

1. In this experiment, you were required to follow a detailed multi-step procedure. How well did you achieve this?

....

....

....

2. You also had to explain why you were doing each of those steps. How well could you do that?

....

....

....

Mini vocabulary warm up

Look at these words:

variation   difference   genetic   natural   environmental   adaptation

Which of these:

1. refers to surrounding conditions, such as temperature? ……………………………………….. [1 mark]

2. means inherited characteristics? ....[1 mark]

3. means one organism not being the same as another? ………………………………..…[1 mark]

4. refers to factors that are not the result of human activity? ......…………………...……… [1 mark]

5. means the differences between individual organisms in a species? ………………...............[1 mark]

6. is the process whereby organisms change to fit their environment? ....……..…… [1 mark]

Each of the following statements is either **true** or **false** – choose the correct response.

7. In a litter of puppies, the puppies are similar but not identical.
    This is an example of variation. **True / False**   [1 mark]

8. Arthur grows geraniums in his flowerbeds. He makes sure the soil is rich in nutrients.
    This is an example of controlling the environment. **True / False**   [1 mark]

9. Zena is a keen runner. Her leg muscles are well developed and she can run for
    longer now than she could do a few years ago. This is an example of adaptation.
    True / False   [1 mark]

10. Will's class is exploring variation in height. They measure all their classmates' heights, add up the
    measurements and divide the answer by the number of students. This calculation will show the
    variation in height in the class members. **True / False**   [1 mark]

11. Juanita's group have been growing broad beans from seeds to investigate how they vary. They
    have been running the experiment for several weeks and observe different features.

| Juanita: The plants have grown to different heights but we grew them in different pots and we didn't make sure they all had the same amount of water. I think the variation might be due to different conditions. | Michelle: Variation seems to affect some things and not others. They have grown to different heights but all the plants have the same number of leaves. | Emile: We can't really tell yet if they do vary in height. Some are taller but they're all still growing. We need to let them reach their full height; they might all grow to the same height eventually. |

Write a response to each of these ideas:

    a. Juanita: .... [1 mark]

    b. Michelle: .... [1 mark]

    c. Emile: ....[1 mark]

Purpose of practical activity

In this experiment you will study variation – focusing on cress seedlings. All living things exhibit variation. If you look at students in a classroom or daisies growing in a meadow, variation is always present. Organisms may be similar, but they are rarely identical.

Learning outcomes	Maths skills required
• To investigate how variation is displayed in seedlings. • To gather and analyse data to support conclusions. • To explore how scientific explanations may bring about changes in understanding.	• To take and record measurements. • To use central measures, such as the mean, median and mode, to analyse data. • To identify and deal with outliers.

Set up

Apparatus list
• Potting compost • Seed trays   (Note: cress seed can also be grown in damp cotton wool in plastic tubs.) • Cress seed • Rulers • Calculators

Safety notes
• *Wash your hands with soap and water after handling the compost and seeds, and after clearing up. Do not taste any of the seeds.*

Common mistakes and how to avoid them
• When taking measurements of height, remember it is the height above ground level and not the total length of the seedling that is being used. • Remember to distinguish between mean, median and mode. • Seedlings need water but excess water will swamp the plants and may rot the seeds or roots.

Method

Read these instructions carefully before you start work.

Part 1: Growing the seeds

1. Set up a seed tray with a shallow layer of compost and sprinkle around 40–50 cress seeds on top, fairly evenly distributed.

2. Sprinkle water over the tray to moisten the compost but do not allow it to become saturated.

3. Label the tray to identify it as the one that your group set up.

4. Leave for several days to allow the seeds to germinate and grow, but check occasionally to ensure the compost has not dried out.

Part 2: Measuring the seedlings

1. After the seedlings have grown to a height of 2–3 cm you can take measurements to gather evidence.

2. You need to record the height of each seedling. Start at one side of the tray, measure the height of a seedling, record it and remove it from the tray so that you can reach the next one (and so that you will not measure that one twice). Continue until you have the heights of all the seedlings. Retain the seedlings for further examination.

Results

Record the height of each seedling in these columns (you can use each column for a number of values).

Analyse results

1. First, you need to identify any outliers. These are measurements that are either much less or much greater than the others. The seedlings are likely to look less healthy or to be in some way different from the others (not just in height). How many of these seedlings were there?

   ....

2. Now find the mean height by adding up all the heights, counting all the seedlings and dividing the total height by this number. Show your working and remember to include units.

   ....

   ....

3. Now find the median. To do this, the heights need to be in ascending order. A good way of doing this is to set up a tally chart. Head a column with each of the heights, starting with the lowest. For example, if the height of the shortest seedling was 1.8 cm put that in the first column heading, 1.9 cm in the next heading, and so on. Then put a tick in each column for each seedling of that height.

Height												
No. of seedlings of that height												

   Find the median by halving the total number of seedlings and counting along the ticks in the table, starting from the left, until you reach that number. ....

4. From the table, find the mode (the most common height). ....

5. What was the difference between the tallest and the shortest (once the outliers had been removed)? Show your working and remember to include units.

   ....

6. Which of these statements is the best fit for your results?

   a. The seedlings showed no variation at all in height.

   b. The seedlings showed some variation but not a great deal.

   c. The seedlings showed a large amount of variation.

   State which one you selected and why.

   ....

Check your understanding

1. Gina's group have completed their experiment and are discussing their results.

Gina: There's no difference in height between the seedlings. I know the results show some differences but that's only because we were trying to measure from the compost, which was not level.	Emile: There was a lot of difference in height.	Zena: I think there was some difference. It wasn't huge but some were clearly taller than others.

   Who do you think was right and why?

   ....

   .... [1 mark]

2. Juanita's group are discussing which calculations are useful. Juanita says, 'The mean isn't very helpful because, for example, we have four dogs at home; three of them are about 30 cm tall and the other one is much bigger, about 90 cm tall. The mean is 45 cm but there is no dog 45 cm tall. The mode and the median are both 30 cm and that's sensible. That's the height of most of our dogs.'

   a. How relevant do you think Juanita's comment is to your data?

   .... [1 mark]

   b. Out of the mean, median and mode, which do you think is the most useful when indicating how tall your seedlings grew?

   .... [1 mark]

Spot the mistake

1. Will's group found the mean height by pulling all the seedlings out of the compost, laying them out on the bench and measuring the total length of each plant. Why was this a mistake?

   ....

   .... [1 mark]

2. Michelle's group did not keep their seedlings moist and so most dried out and died. They retrieved five or six 'survivors' and used these for their measurements. Why was this a mistake?

....

.... [1 mark]

3. After completing the experiment, Kareem's group concluded, 'All of the seedlings should have been the same height because they were the same plant variety, grown under identical conditions. The differences recorded were due to inaccuracies in measuring.' Why was this a mistake?

....

.... [1 mark]

Apply your understanding

1. Seedlings may vary in other ways than just height.

    a. Look at the root length in your seedlings – is there any variation? .... [1 mark]

    b. Examine the seedlings. Do taller seedlings have longer roots? .... [1 mark]

2. For a seedling, why might being a little taller be

    a. an advantage? .... [1 mark]

    b. a disadvantage? .... [1 mark]

3. For a seedling, why might being a little shorter be:

    a. an advantage? .... [1 mark]

    b. a disadvantage? .... [1 mark]

Evaluate your learning

1. In this experiment you had to process a lot of data. How well do you think you managed this?

....

....

2. How well do you think you've understood the concept of variation?

....

....

Mini vocabulary warm up

Look at these words: **quadrat factors hypothesis correlation transect**

Which of these:

1. is the square apparatus that is used to mark out a section of ground? .... [1 mark]

2. are things that might affect whether an organism inhabits an area? .... [1 mark]

3. refers to a situation in which two factors vary in a similar way? ……...........................…[1 mark]

4. refers to an idea about a relationship between variables that is supported by scientific thinking but needs to be tested?

   .... [1 mark]

5. is a line along which observations are made of the population of an organism?

   .... [1 mark]

Look at these words relating to managing sets of data:

sampling mean median mode percentage

Which of these:

6. is used to find out how common an organism is in an area, without having to count every one?

   .... [1 mark]

7. is the proportion of the area of a quadrat that is covered by an organism?...................... [1 mark]

8. is found by adding up a set of data values and dividing by how many of these values there are?

   .... [1 mark]

9. is found by sorting numbers into increasing order and finding the halfway value?

   .... [1 mark]

10. is the value that appears most frequently in a group? .... [1 mark]

11. Emile's group are investigating if flat-leaf plants are more common on the school football pitch than in grass on the rest of the school grounds. They have decided to work out the percentage cover in six quadrats on the playing field and in six quadrats on the rest of the grass.

Emile: The experiment won't work unless we find some flat-leaf plants. We need to see where they are so we can put the quadrats there.	Kareem: We should throw the quadrats so they land in random places.	Michelle: We should put the quadrats in a neat row at measured intervals.

    Who do you think is right, and why?

    ....[2 marks]

Purpose of practical activity

Fieldwork involves gathering evidence to answer questions about habitats. The data might include taking measurements or making observations, and should enable conclusions to be drawn – these should reflect the fact that in fieldwork there is no control over the independent variables. We might think, for example, that a certain plant will grow better where it is damp, but damp places may also be colder and darker. Nevertheless, we can learn much about living organisms from well-planned and executed fieldwork. In this activity you will investigate if the incidence of dandelion plants varies in different parts of a grassed area by exploring whether there is a relationship between the distance from a particular feature in the grounds and the size of the dandelion population.

Learning outcomes	Maths skills required
<ul><li>To plan and carry out a fieldwork investigation.</li><li>To use sampling techniques to gather data.</li><li>To draw conclusions that are valid.</li></ul>	<ul><li>Identify patterns and trends in data.</li><li>Calculation of mean, median and mode.</li></ul>

Set up

Apparatus list		
• Quadrats	• Clipboards	• Tape measures

Safety notes
<ul><li>*When doing fieldwork, wear suitable clothing and footwear especially in wet, muddy conditions. Follow your teacher's instructions and be aware of any poisonous, stinging or irritant plants where you are working.*</li><li>*You should not eat or drink during fieldwork until you have finished the activity and have washed your hands. (Use a cleaning wipe or hand gel if there are no handwashing facilities.)*</li><li>*Any cuts or broken skin should be covered by a waterproof dressing before doing fieldwork. Any cuts sustained during fieldwork should be reported to your teacher for cleaning and treatment*</li></ul>

Common mistakes and how to avoid them
<ul><li>If you are placing a quadrat a certain distance from a feature, measure the distance to the middle of the quadrat, not to the edge.</li><li>It can be difficult to distinguish one plant from another, especially if there are quite a few types present. Ensure you are familiar with the characteristics of a dandelion (maybe use an identification guide) and also clearly separate any plants.</li><li>Do not be tempted to position the transect line where there are more dandelions; your data should be typical of the whole area.</li></ul>

Method

Read these instructions carefully before you start work.

1. You are investigating dandelion plants, so make sure you are familiar with their appearance – key features are bright yellow flowers, deeply-notched hairless leaves and a hollow stem.

2. As a group, identify an environment feature that you think could make a difference to how dandelions grow. This could be a building, a bank, a hedge or a foootpath.

3. Now develop an idea about whether dandelions might be more common, less common or unaffected by this feature. Suggest why this might be. Be clear about your reasoning.

4. Use quadrats to mark out a sample area to count the plants. Go to the feature you have selected and run out the tape measure in a straight line. Decide where you are going to place the quadrats. For example, if the feature is a hedge and you have quadrats of 0.5 m by 0.5 m, you could place quadrats every 1 m for a total of 9 m moving away from the hedge.

5. Now looking at the ground within the quadrat, count the number of dandelion plants and record this. Make a note of the distance of the quadrat from the feature. It is also good practice to make a note of any other features in the area that might make a difference. For example, you might be moving away from the hedge but getting closer to a large tree. Record your results.

6. Repeat with each of the quadrats, recording your results each time.

Results

Quadrat number	1	2	3	4	5	6	7	8	9
Distance from key feature (m)									
Number of plants in quadrat									
Other significant features									

Analyse results

1. a. What was the feature that your group investigated? ………………………………………

   b. Explain what difference you thought this might make to the dandelion population, and why.

   ……

2. Look at the numbers of plants you found in each quadrat.

   a. What was the mean number of plants you found in the survey? …………………………

   b. What was the median number of plants you found in the survey? ………………………

   c. What was the value of the mode for the plants you found? …………………………………

Check your understanding

1. Why it is necessary to use quadrats and not count all the plants in an area?

   ……………………………………………………………………………………………………… [1 mark]

2. Why is it a good idea to note any other significant features in an area?

   ……………………………………………………………………………………………………… [1 mark]

Spot the mistake

1. Zena's group counted the dandelion flowers and recorded this as the number of plants. Why was this a mistake?

   .... [1 mark]

2. Emile's group looked for patches of dandelions, put the quadrats around them, counted the plants and measured the distance from the quadrat to the feature. Why was this a mistake?

   .... [1 mark]

Apply your understanding

1. Juanita's group hypothesised that daisies prefer full sun and so fewer will grow near a hedge than in open ground. They measured the distance from the base of a hedge and, at each point, put a quadrat down and counted the daisy plants in the quadrat. Here are their results.

Distance from the hedge (m)	1	2	3	4	5	6	7	8	9
Number of daisy plants in quadrat	3	4	7	8	7	8	6	9	7

   a. What was the mean number of plants in a quadrat? ....[1 mark]

   b. What was the median number of plants in a quadrat? .... [1 mark]

   c. What was the modal number of plants in a quadrat? .... [1 mark]

   d. What do the results show?

   ....[2 marks]

   e. Do the results support the group's hypothesis?

   ....[2 marks]

2. Zena's group are investigating the hypothesis that the number of seagulls in the schoolyard is greatest immediately following break and lunchtimes. Suggest how this could be investigated.

   ....

   ....[3 marks]

Evaluate your learning

1. Gathering data outdoors is not always easy. What challenges did you encounter and how did you overcome them?

   ....

2. What would you do differently if you had to repeat the investigation?

   ....

   ....

Mini vocabulary warm up

Look at these words:

acid   alkali   salt   water   neutralise   evaporation   crystallisation   base

Which of these:

1. has a pH of less than 7? .... [1 mark]

2. will neutralise an acid? .... [1 mark]

3. involves turning a liquid into a vapour? .... [1 mark]

4. is a technique used to separate solids dissolved in liquids?................................. [1 mark]

5. in Chemistry, means 'to cancel out'? .... [1 mark]

6. has a pH of more than 7 and is insoluble?.. [1 mark]

Each of the following statements is either **true** or **false** – choose the correct response.

7. There is a group of chemicals called salts – salt is not just one substance. **True / False**   [1 mark]

8. The chemical name for common table salt is sodium chloride. **True / False**   [1 mark]

9. Magnesium sulfate is a compound. **True / False**   [1 mark]

10. Magnesium sulfate contains metal. **True / False**   [1 mark]

11. Neutralisation means always using equal volumes of an acid and an alkali. **True / False**   [1 mark]

12. Neutralisation involves passing an electric current through chemicals. **True / False**   [1 mark]

13. Juanita's group are investigating salt. They have made some salt by neutralising hydrochloric acid with sodium hydroxide.

Juanita: These crystals of salt must be safe for us to taste; after all, we made them by neutralising the acid so the pH must be 7.

Gina: Even if it was clean, we might not have got the neutralisation spot on. There might be a bit of acid or alkali left.

Zena: I don't think that's a good idea. The apparatus isn't necessarily clean.

What do you think about their ideas?

....

....

....[3 marks]

Purpose of practical activity

In this experiment you will be using magnesium carbonate, an insoluble base, which you will react with sulfuric acid to make crystals of magnesium sulfate. There are several stages to the procedure and it is important that you understand each stage, to be able to complete the experiment effectively. First, you will react the reactants, then filter the liquid and finally evaporate water to leave the crystals. If you are successful, you should get a good yield of colourless crystals called Epsom salts.

Learning outcomes	Maths skills required
<ul><li>Follow a procedure to produce a chemical.</li><li>Apply the concepts of acids and alkalis to explain a process.</li><li>Use a range of laboratory equipment safely.</li></ul>	<ul><li>Relate the characteristics of types of chemicals to a numerical scale.</li></ul>

Set up

Apparatus list

- Beakers (e.g. 100 ml)
- Conical flasks (e.g. 100 ml)
- Spatulas
- Glass stirring rods
- Evaporating basins
- Crystallising dishes
- Filter funnels and filter papers
- pH indicator paper
- Heating apparatus, including gauze
- Sulfuric acid, 0.5 M
- Magnesium carbonate
- 50 ml measuring cylinders
- Hand lenses
- Eye protection

Safety notes

- *Always be careful when handling chemicals and follow your teacher's safety advice about sulfuric acid and magnesium carbonate (see CLEAPSS guidance).*
- *Wear eye protection during all practical activity and until everyone has finished clearing up.*
- *Avoid skin contact with the acid, especially when it is hot, and do not let the acid mixture boil dry.*
- *Do not let the evaporating basin boil dry or hot material will 'spit' out and burn you.*

Common mistakes and how to avoid them

- Ensure that the reaction in the first stage is complete by checking whether any more magnesium carbonate will react and that you have a neutral solution.
- The filtration should be completed before the solution cools to room temperature – but not when it is too hot to handle.
- In the evaporation stage, do not boil the basin dry when heating with the Bunsen burner.

Method

Read these instructions carefully before you start work.

1. Measure 50 ml of sulfuric acid into a measuring cylinder and pour it into the beaker. Use a spatula to add small amounts of magnesium carbonate, stirring each time until it is dissolved.

2. When no more magnesium carbonate dissolves, heat the beaker **gently** for a few minutes to ensure the reaction is complete. Then remove the heat. If the resulting mixture is clear, stir in more magnesium carbonate until the mixture is cloudy.

3. Now use indicator paper to check the pH of the solution; it should be neutral. If it isn't, continue adding and stirring in magnesium carbonate until it is dissolved.

4. Place the filter funnel in the flask and set up the filter paper. The paper is circular; fold it to form a semicircle and again to form a quarter circle. This has four layers; open it to form a cone so that there are three layers on one side and one on the other. It will now fit in the funnel.

5. Make sure the beaker is cool enough to hold at the top. The contents should still be hot.

6. Swirl the contents gently to make sure all the solid material will be carried through and pour them into the filter paper. If the solution in the flask has any solid in it, repeat the filtration.

7. Pour the clear solution into an evaporating basin and place on the gauze on the tripod.

8. Heat the solution so that the water boils steadily but **do not boil it dry**. When about half the water has boiled away, take a drop on a glass rod and let it cool – if this crystallises, the solution is ready for the next stage; if it does not crystallise, keep boiling and repeating the test until the drop crystallises.

9. Pour the solution into a crystallising dish and leave to cool, with a label showing the name of your group.

10. If necessary, filter the solution, collect the crystals from the filter paper onto a paper towel and allow to dry. Use a hand lens to analyse the crystals.

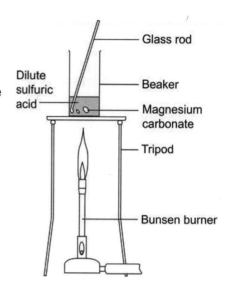

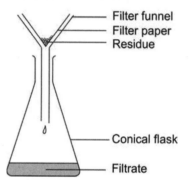

Results

1. In the box below, draw a few examples of the crystals you see through the hand lens.

Analyse results

1. Why was it necessary:

   a. for the sulfuric acid to be hot?

   .... [1 mark]

   b. for the solution to be filtered?

   .... [1 mark]

   c. to avoid boiling the mixture dry?

   .... [1 mark]

Check your understanding

1. What is a salt?

   .... [1 mark]

2. What is the difference between an alkali and a base?

   ....

   .... [1 mark]

3. What is distinctive about the shape of crystals?

   ....

   ....[2 marks]

Spot the mistake

1. During one group's experiment, some fumes are produced. What do you think they are doing wrong?

   ....

   ....

   .... [1 mark]

2. Michelle's group completed the experiment and managed to get several crystals. There were other bits of solid in the crystallising dish. What do you think might have happened?

   ....

   ....

   .... [1 mark]

Apply your understanding

1. Magnesium carbonate is insoluble in water. Why do you think it dissolves in warm acid?

   ....

   ....

   .... [1 mark]

2. If all the magnesium carbonate disappeared, you added more. What effect did this have on the pH of the mixture?

   ....

   ....

   .... [1 mark]

3. What do you think would happen if you added water to the crystals?

   ....

   ....

   .... [1 mark]

Evaluate your learning

1. In doing this experiment, you needed not only to follow instructions but also to understand why you were doing the various stages. How well do you think you did this?

   ....

   ....

   ....

2. Safety is a key consideration in this experiment. How did you make sure everyone in your group was kept safe?

   ....

   ....

   ....

Mini vocabulary warm up

Look at these words:

oxygen   copper   lead   carbon dioxide   metal oxide   charcoal

Which of these:

1. are metals? ………………………………………… and ……………………………………[2 marks]

2. are compounds? ……………………………………… and ……………………………………[2 marks]

3. is a form of carbon? …………………………………………………………………………[1 mark]

4. is a gas that will extinguish a flame? ……………………………………………………..[1 mark]

5. is a gas that will relight a glowing splint? ………………………………………………[1 mark]

Each of the following statements is either **true** or **false** – choose the correct response.

6. Copper is a metal that is good at conducting electricity. **True / False**   [1 mark]

7. Carbon is an element that will form a compound with oxygen. **True / False**   [1 mark]

8. If you heat most metals, they will form an oxide. **True / False**   [1 mark]

9. Some metals are more reactive than others. **True / False**   [1 mark]

10. Carbon catches fire if you heat it strongly enough. **True / False**   [1 mark]

Refer to the reactivity list on the right to answer the following questions.

| **Reactivity list** |
| Potassium (most reactive) |
| Sodium |
| Lithium |
| Calcium |
| Magnesium |
| Aluminium |
| Carbon |
| Zinc |
| Iron |
| Tin |
| Lead |
| Copper |
| Silver |
| Gold (least reactive) |

11. Which is more reactive – zinc or tin? ………………………………….[1 mark]

12. Which is more reactive – carbon or lead? …………………………..... [1 mark]

13. Which is more reactive – carbon or copper? ………………………….[1 mark]

14. Which is more reactive – lead or copper? …………………………..... [1 mark]

15. Why is steel not on this list? …………………………………………[1 mark]

16. Zena's group are studying a picture of the death mask of the Egyptian Pharaoh Tutankhamun. When the mask was found, the gold was shiny even though it was about 5000 years old.

Zena: It was still shiny because it stayed dry. Metals go rusty when they get wet.

Will: It was still shiny because gold is very unreactive. It's when metals react with other things that they lose their shine.

Emile: It must have been polished – nothing stays shiny for thousands of years.

Who do you think is right and why?

………

…………………………………………………………………………………………………[2 marks]

Purpose of practical activity

This experiment will introduce you to extracting metals from their ores. An ore is a substance that contains a metal but the metal has reacted with something else. To get the pure metal the other substances have to be removed.

In this experiment you will be extracting two metals – lead and copper. You will extract lead from lead oxide by heating the lead oxide with charcoal, which is made from carbon. Due to the fact that carbon is more reactive than lead it will remove the oxygen from the lead oxide, forming carbon dioxide (which escapes as a gas) and will leave the lead behind. You will extract copper from copper oxide, again by heating it with charcoal to form copper and carbon dioxide.

Learning outcomes		
• Understand how metals can be extracted.	• Follow a procedure with due regard for safety.	• Observe the outcomes of reactions

Set up

Apparatus list	
• Copper (II) oxide (1 g per test) • Lead (II) oxide (1 g per test) • Charcoal (2 g per test) • Bunsen burners • Eye protection • Heat-resistant mat • Crucibles	• Hard glass test tubes (ignition tubes) • Test-tube holders • Test-tube racks (preferably metal not wooden) • Spatulas • Plastic weighing dishes (boats) • Pipe clay triangles • Sand bucket

Safety notes
• *Always be careful when handling chemicals and follow your teacher's safety advice about copper (II) oxide, lead (II) oxide and charcoal (see CLEAPSS guidance).* • *Avoid skin contact with the oxides and don't raise any dust from them.* • *Wear eye protection when doing all the practical activities and until everyone has finished clearing up.* • *Take care not to burn yourself with hot test tubes. Put them on the mat or in a metal rack to cool – not on the bench.* • *Test tubes may break under intense heat, so make sure you know what to do in such cases. It is a good idea to have a sand bucket available.*

Common mistakes and how to avoid them
• Charcoal and copper oxide look similar – it is easy to get them mixed up. • It is easier to see if a reaction has occurred if you use small quantities.

Method

Read these instructions carefully before you start work.

Experiment 1: extracting lead

1. Put one spatula (1 g) measure of lead (II) oxide on the empty weighing dish or boat.

2. Add one spatula (2 g) measure of charcoal powder to the dish.

3. Use the spatula to mix them together.

4. Carefully put the mixture into a hard glass test tube and heat the tube strongly for 5 minutes in a Bunsen flame.

5. Allow the test tube to cool in its holder on a heat-resistant mat.

6. Tip the cooled mixture out onto the heat-resistant mat and examine it.

Alternatively:

1. Put the lead oxide (1 g) and the charcoal (2 g) into a crucible and mix using the spatula.

2. Put the crucible onto a pipe clay triangle on a tripod and heat for 10−15 minutes.

3. Allow to cool.

4. Tip the cooled mixture out onto the heat-resistant mat and examine it.

Experiment 2: extracting copper

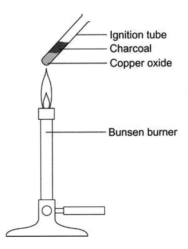

1. Put one spatula (1 g) measure of copper (II) oxide into a hard glass test tube.

2. Carefully add one spatula (2 g) of charcoal powder on top of the copper oxide without any mixing.

3. Strongly heat these two layers for 5 minutes in a Bunsen flame.

4. Allow to cool and then look closely at where the powders meet in the test tube.

Results

1. Make notes in this box, using words and drawings about the products you saw forming in Experiment 1 (extracting lead).

2. Make notes in this box, using words and drawings about the products you could see formed in Experiment 2 (extracting copper).

Analyse results

1. Think about the results. What evidence was there for the formation of a metal in each case?

   ....

   ....[2 marks]

2. The word equation for the extraction of lead is:

   lead oxide (....) + carbon (....) → lead (....) + carbon dioxide (....)

   In the brackets after each substance, write **s, l or g** to show the state of matter.   [1 mark]

3. Write the word equation for the reaction of copper oxide and charcoal indicating whether the substances are s, l or g.

   .... [1 mark]

Check your understanding

1. In each experiment, why was a metal produced?

   ....

   ....[2 marks]

2. In each experiment:

   a. what was the other product in addition to the metal? .... [1 mark]

   b. what happened to this other product? .... [1 mark]

Spot the mistake

1. Kareem's group mixed the powdered copper oxide and charcoal together before heating them. Why was this a mistake?

   ....

   .... [1 mark]

2. Gina's group heated the tube in each experiment for about a minute and then stopped. Why was this a mistake?

   ....

   .... [1 mark]

3. Michelle's group used an ordinary test tube instead of an ignition tube for the lead oxide and charcoal experiment. Why was this a mistake?

   ....

   .... [1 mark]

Apply your understanding

1. If carbon (in the form of charcoal) is heated with tin oxide, it will remove the oxygen from the tin and form carbon dioxide. If, however, charcoal is heated with aluminium oxide, there is no reaction. Use the reactivity list to explain why.

   ....

   ....[2 marks]

2. a. From which metals in the reactivity list will charcoal remove oxygen from the metal oxide?

   .... [1 mark]

   b. Explain your answer.

   ....

   .... [1 mark]

3. Charcoal is not used to remove oxygen from gold oxide to produce gold. Explain why not.

   ....

   ....[1 mark]

4. We can use chemical equations to represent these lead oxide and copper oxide reactions. The equations are shown below but are incomplete. Complete both equations by rewriting them, inserting their states of matter and balancing them.

   a. $PbO + C \rightarrow Pb + CO_2$

   ....[1 mark]

   b. $CuO + C \rightarrow Cu + CO_2$

   ....[1 mark]

Evaluate your learning

1. In this experiment, you made chemicals react to make metals. How well did you do this?

   ....

   ....

2. This experiment uses hazardous materials and high temperatures. How did you avoid any accidents?

   ....

   ....

   ....

Mini vocabulary warm up

Look at these words:

reaction   reactants   products   rate   excess   complete

Which of these: (Note: each word may be used more than once.)

1. represents chemicals produced during a reaction? ....[1 mark]

2. indicates that more of a chemical has been provided than can be used up in the reaction?

    .... [1 mark]

3. takes place and causes products to be made? ....[1 mark]

4. indicates that no further reaction will take place? ....[1 mark]

5. relates to how quickly the reaction is happening? ....[1 mark]

6. represents chemicals used up during a reaction? ....[1 mark]

7. If a gas is made during a reaction, it can be collected and tested. Match these gases to the correct test.   [3 marks]

Hydrogen
Carbon dioxide
Oxygen

Extinguishes a flame
Relights a glowing splint
Burns with a squeaky pop

Each of the following statements is either **true** or **false** – choose the correct response.

8. Magnesium is a metal. **True / False**   [1 mark]

9. Reactions always produce a gas. **True / False**   [1 mark]

10. When a reaction mixture bubbles, it means a gas is being formed. **True / False**   [1 mark]

11. There has to be acid present for a reaction to take place. **True / False**   [1 mark]

12. Burning is a type of reaction. **True / False**   [1 mark]

13. Reactions always produce heat. **True / False**   [1 mark]

14. Zena is making a cake with her friends.

> Zena: Baking a cake isn't a chemical reaction – it doesn't use any chemicals!

> Emile: The cake mix is a liquid and baking it makes it go solid. It's a physical change like when water freezes to form ice.

> Will: Baking a cake is a chemical reaction. Once you've baked it, you can't get back to the ingredients you started with.

    a. Who is correct? .... [1 mark]

    b. Explain your reasoning.

       .... [1 mark]

Purpose of practical activity

In this experiment, you will be investigating the reaction between sulfuric acid and magnesium and, in particular, how the concentration of the acid affects the rate of reaction. These chemicals react to form magnesium sulfate and hydrogen.

Learning outcomes	Maths skills required
• Understand how to use equipment and chemicals to produce a chemical reaction and gather the gas produced. • Use different concentrations of acid and relate this to the amount of gas produced. • Gather data and use to support conclusions.	• Gather and tabulate data. • Draw a graph showing the relationship between two variables. • Recognise and interpret graphs that illustrate trends.

Set up

Apparatus list

- Conical flasks with delivery tubes
- Water troughs
- Sulfuric acid (different concentrations, e.g. 1 M, 0.75 M, 0.5 M and 0.25 M)
- 50 ml measuring cylinders
- Magnesium ribbon (cut into 3 cm strips)
- Eye protection
- Test tubes
- Timers

Safety notes

- *Always be careful when handling chemicals and follow your teacher's safety advice about sulfuric acid and magnesium carbonate (see CLEAPSS guidance).*
- *Wear eye protection during all practical activity and until everyone has finished clearing up.*
- *Avoid skin contact with the acids.*
- *There must be no naked flames in the lab while the hydrogen gas is being generated..*

Common mistakes and how to avoid them

- The reaction will start as soon as the magnesium contacts the acid. It is important that the delivery tube and timer are ready, and the inverted test tube is full of water before the magnesium is put into the acid.

Method

Read these instructions carefully before you start work.

1. Measure 25 ml of sulfuric acid into the conical flask.

2. Set up the delivery tube, trough and test tube. The test tube should be inverted and full of water. These need to be ready because the reaction will start as soon as the magnesium ribbon contacts the acid. Have a timer ready.

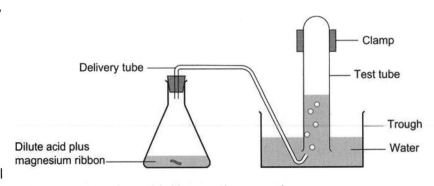

3. Put one piece of magnesium ribbon into the acid and immediately insert the bung in the neck of the flask and start timing. It may be necessary to give the flask a quick swirl to ensure all of the magnesium ribbon reacts with the acid.

4. The reaction will produce hydrogen. Time how long it takes to fill the test tube with gas. Record the time against the concentration of the acid in the table.

5. Remove the bung, empty and rinse out the flask.

6. Refill with the same volume of sulfuric acid of a different concentration, refill the test tube with water, reset the arrangement and be ready to start a new test.

7. Add the magnesium and start the reaction. When the test tube is full, record the results.

8. Reset and repeat for other concentrations of sulfuric acid

Results

1. Record your results in this table.

Concentration of sulfuric acid used (M)	Time taken to produce a test tube full of gas (s)

2. Now plot the results on this graph paper.

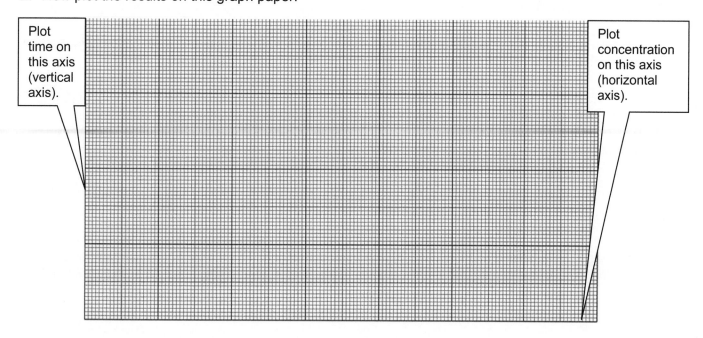

Plot time on this axis (vertical axis).

Plot concentration on this axis (horizontal axis).

Analyse results

1. Looking at your graph:

    a. what is the independent variable? .... [1 mark]

    b. what is the dependent variable? .... [1 mark]

2. Kareem says 'if the concentration is doubled, the gas should be produced in half the time.' Is he correct? Why?

    ....[2 marks]

3. How do your results compare with those of other groups in the class?

    ....

    ....

Check your understanding

1. Why was it important to keep the volume of acid the same for the different acid concentrations?

    .... [1 mark]

2. Why was it important to have the equipment ready before adding the magnesium to the acid?

    .... [1 mark]

3. Why is there a limit to the accuracy of the results that you can get from this experiment?

    ....

    ....[3 marks]

Spot the mistake

1. Michelle's group set up the experiment and collected gas from the reaction. They then held the test tube with the open mouth upwards before trying to ignite it. Why was there no reaction?

    .... [1 mark]

2. Kareem says, 'There is no need to rinse out the flask between experiments because each time sulfuric acid and magnesium are being used.' Why is this a mistake?

    ....

    .... [1 mark]

3. Zena says, 'The graph is wrong because the axes are wrong. The independent variable always goes on the horizontal axis and time is always independent of anything else'. Why is she wrong?

    ....

    .... [1 mark]

Apply your understanding

1. The word equation for this reaction is:

   sulfuric acid + magnesium → magnesium sulfate + hydrogen

   a. What would the products have been if the acid used was nitric acid?

   ....[2 marks]

   b. What would the products have been if the reaction had been between sulfuric acid and calcium?

   ....[2 marks]

2. Magnesium sulfate is a salt. Another salt is sodium chloride.

   a. Which acid and which metal react to produce sodium chloride?

   ....[2 marks]

   b. Why is this not a reaction that school students would be asked to try out? (Hint: You may need to do a bit of research here.)

   .... [1 mark]

3. How can you use your graph to suggest what the concentration of 25 ml of sulfuric acid should be to produce a test tube full of hydrogen in exactly 2 minutes?

   ....

   ....[2 marks]

Evaluate your learning

1. To do this experiment well, you had to work as a team to use the equipment effectively and safely to gather good-quality data. How well do you think you did this?

   ....

   ....

2. How could you adapt the method to see if the pattern found applies to other acid concentrations?

   ....

   ....

Mini vocabulary warm up

Look at these words:

reaction   reactants   products   rate   complete   catalyst

Which of these:

1. means the materials consumed in a chemical reaction? ………………………………..……… [1 mark]

2. means the materials produced in a chemical reaction? ……………………………….. [1 mark]

3. is the process by which new chemicals are produced? ……………………………….. [1 mark]

4. refers to how quickly a reaction has taken place? ………………………………………... [1 mark]

5. refers to when all the reactants have been used up? ……………………………….. [1 mark]

6. is something that will speed up a chemical reaction? ……………………………….. [1 mark]

Each of the following statements is either **true or false** – choose the correct response.

7. When a reaction takes place, there is always heat given off. **True / False**   [1 mark]

8. Heat always has to be supplied to start a chemical reaction. **True / False**   [1 mark]

9. There are always two reactants in a chemical reaction. **True / False**   [1 mark]

10. There are always two products from a chemical reaction. **True / False**   [1 mark]

11. A catalyst speeds up or slows down a chemical reaction. **True / False**   [1 mark]

12. A catalyst is not used up in a chemical reaction. **True / False**   [1 mark]

13. Will's group are discussing whether striking a match is a chemical reaction.

Will: Striking a match is a chemical reaction because you end up with a burned match and you can't get back to the unburnt match.

Kareem: It's not a chemical reaction because the match is not reacting with anything – it's just a match.

Juanita: It's a chemical reaction because heat is given off. Energy transfers always mean a chemical reaction has occurred.

   a. What do you think about their ideas?

   ....

   ....[3 marks]

   b. If you were in their group, what would you say?

   ....

   ....[2 marks]

Purpose of practical activity

In this experiment you are going to be exploring the effect of three different catalysts on the decomposition of hydrogen peroxide. This naturally decomposes to water by releasing oxygen. Catalysts can alter the rate at which a reaction takes place. By adding washing-up liquid to the hydrogen peroxide, we can see the oxygen being released. It will be up to you, however, to decide what evidence to gather to compare the catalysts fairly.

Learning outcomes	Maths skills required
<ul><li>Design a procedure to gather evidence.</li><li>Gather evidence to support a conclusion.</li><li>Evaluate the procedure.</li></ul>	<ul><li>To gather and tabulate evidence and present data in charts.</li></ul>

Set up

Apparatus list

- Hydrogen peroxide solution (10 vol, 3%) (10 ml per catalyst) (this may be diluted prior to experiment if desired)
- 100 ml measuring cylinders
- Large trays
- A variety of catalysts to test, for example, small pieces of liver (or yeast), apple and potato
- A small amount of washing-up liquid
- Splints

- Tweezers to handle the solids
- Dropping pipettes
- Eye protection
- Disposal bins
- Equipment to measure the reaction between the hydrogen peroxide and the catalysts, for example, rulers for measuring the size of oxygen bubbles produced, timers for measuring speed of reaction, smartphones or tablets with video apps.

Safety notes

- *Avoid skin contact with the hydrogen peroxide.*
- *Wear eye protection when doing all the practical activities and until everyone has finished clearing up.*
- *Do not taste any of the substances and wash your hands when you have finished.*
- *Keep the measuring cylinder in a tray to catch any spills.*

Common mistakes and how to avoid them

- Oxygen can be formed quickly, so it is important to be ready to measure the height of any rising bubbles, if that is the measurement being made.
- It is important to measure the time taken from the start to the maximum height of bubbles being produced accurately, if that is the measurement being made.

Method

Read these instructions carefully before you start work.

1. Start by viewing a teacher demonstration of the decomposition of hydrogen peroxide. Notice how the washing-up liquid froths up as the oxygen is released.

2. You are going to explore the effect of using three different materials as catalysts (for example, liver or yeast, apple and potato). To compare these effectively you will be gathering evidence; it is important to make this comparison a fair test. As a group, decide what evidence you need (what measurements you will be taking) and how to ensure the comparisons are fair.

3. Begin the experiment by placing 10 ml of hydrogen peroxide into the measuring cylinder and adding a few drops of washing-up liquid.

4. Now add the first catalyst and record the measurements you have decided to take. You will need to make a table – discuss as a group what columns to use.

5. When the reaction is over, tip away the contents into a disposal bin, rinse out the cylinder, put in fresh hydrogen peroxide and test the next catalyst.

6. Repeat until you have tested all the catalysts and you have recorded a full set of results.

Results

1. Set out a table to show the catalysts you tested and the measurements you took.

2. Use the grid below to draw a bar chart displaying your results.

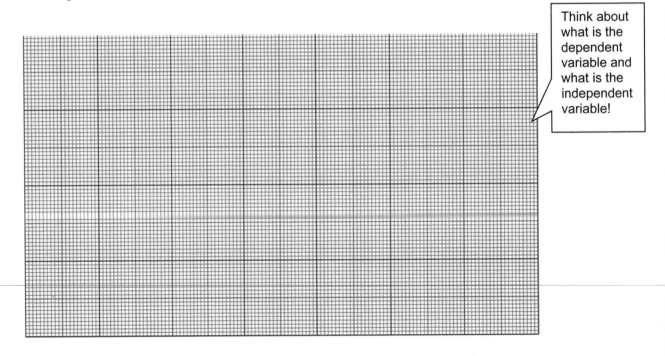

Think about what is the dependent variable and what is the independent variable!

Analyse results

1. According to your results:

    a. which was the most effective catalyst?...

    b. which was the least effective catalyst?..

2. Each of the materials tested works as a catalyst, because they contain a chemical called catalase. Some of the materials have more catalase than others. What can you say about the amount of catalase in each of the catalysts you tested?

    ....

    ....

3. How did you ensure it was a fair test between the catalysts?

    ....

    ....

Check your understanding

1. Kursad says, 'I think the washing-up liquid was also a catalyst, because without the washing-up liquid there was no bubbling up.' What do you think?

    ....

    .... [1 mark]

2. What is the advantage of using a bar chart to display data compared to a line graph?

    ....

    .... [1 mark]

3. A catalyst affects the rate of a reaction but is not consumed in the reaction.

    a. How could you test whether the catalyst is unchanged at the end of the reaction?

    ....

    ....[2 marks]

    b. Why, in practical terms, might that not be easy in this experiment?

    ....

    ....[2 marks]

Spot the mistake

1. Zena's group decided to measure the effectiveness of the catalysts by measuring the time from adding the catalyst to when the bubbles had completely stopped. Why was this not a good idea?

   ....

   ....[1 mark]

2. Michelle's group thought that, because hydrogen peroxide decomposed into water and oxygen, there was nothing hazardous about it. Why is this a potentially dangerous view?

   ....

   ....[1 mark]

Apply your understanding

1. Many cars have catalytic converters, which cause a reaction between carbon monoxide and nitrous oxide. Without catalytic converters, these gases would be released into the atmosphere. The products of the reaction are carbon dioxide and nitrogen.

   a. Where in a car might you expect to find the catalytic converter? .... [1 mark]

   b. Why do you think this car part is referred to as a 'converter'?

   .... [1 mark]

   c. The catalysts are rhodium and platinum. Why are these not used up when the car travels?

   .... [1 mark]

2. Many products are manufactured using processes involving catalysts – two examples are detergents and margarine. Why do you think that manufacturers are keen to use catalysts?

   ....

   ....[2 marks]

Evaluate your learning

1. In this investigation, you collected evidence in the form of measurements to evaluate the effectiveness of the catalysts. How useful were the measurements you took?

   ....

   ....

2. How well do you think you did in identifying the catalyst with the greatest proportion of catalase?

   ....

   ....

   ....

Mini vocabulary warm up

Look at these words:

salt   crystal   soluble   insoluble   purify   yield

Which of these:

1. means something cannot dissolve? .... [1 mark]

2. is a solid object with flat faces and sharp edges? .... [1 mark]

3. refers the amount of product that can be obtained from a raw material? ....[1 mark]

4. is a compound formed from an acid reacting with a base? .... [1 mark]

5. means something will dissolve? ....[1 mark]

6. refers to the removal of any impurities? ....[1 mark]

Each of the following statements is either **true or false** – choose the correct response.

7. Table salt (sodium chloride) is soluble in water. **True / False**   [1 mark]

8. Sand is soluble in water. **True / False**   [1 mark]

9. Substances dissolved in water can be removed by filtration. **True / False**   [1 mark]

10. Insoluble materials can be removed from water by filtration. **True / False**   [1 mark]

11. Gina, Will and Kursad are hiking across Dartmoor. It is a hot day and they are short of water.

Gina: The water from this stream looks good enough to drink. It's flowing down the hillside and looks nice and clear.

Will: It might have bits of moss and stones in it, but if we filtered it, it would be safe to drink.

Kursad: Filtering it wouldn't make it safe to drink. There could be things dissolved in it that would still be present after filtering.

Who do you think is right and why?

....[2 marks]

12. Emile's group are investigating seawater. They left a sample of seawater in a shallow dish on a window sill for several days. When they returned, the water had gone and there was an off-white solid powder on the dish.

    a. What do you think has happened to the water? .... [1 mark]

    b. What is the solid that is left in the dish? .... [1 mark]

    c. What would happen if they added water to it? .... [1 mark]

    d. How could they have removed the water more quickly?

.... [1 mark]

Purpose of practical activity

Scientists often need to obtain pure materials from sources that contain other substances. To do this they use various techniques to separate the chemicals to obtain a product that is pure, or at least purer than what they started with. The amount of the product obtained is called the yield. This investigation involves purifying a common material and calculating the yield obtained.

Learning outcomes	Maths skills required	Formulae
• Understand how to remove various impurities from a solid by following a set procedure. • Calculate the yield. • Evaluate the procedure to improve the process.	• Take and record readings. • Perform calculations to calculate yield.	$\text{yield} = \dfrac{\text{mass of product}}{\text{mass of raw material}} \times 100\%$

Set up

Apparatus list
• Rock salt (100 g) • Eye protection • Large evaporating basins • Mortars and pestles • Bunsen burners • Glass rods • Electronic balances • Tripods and gauzes • Hand lens • Beakers (250 ml) • Heatproof mats • Metal spatulas • Conical flasks (250 ml) • Filter funnels and filter papers

Safety notes
• *Wear eye protection during the practical activity and until everyone has finished clearing up.* • *Do not let the evaporating basin boil dry or the material will 'spit' out and burn you.* • *Do not handle mains plugs, sockets or switches with wet hands.*

Common mistakes and how to avoid them
• The yield needs to be as high as possible, so care needs to be taken to avoid losing any material. • This is a multi-step procedure − ensure each step is completed before moving on to the next one.

Method

Read these instructions carefully before you start work.

1. Weigh out 100 g of rock salt and record this value.

2. Use a mortar and pestle to grind up the rock salt as finely as possible.

3. Put the ground-up rock salt into a beaker and add water. Stir the mixture and, if needed, warm the solution to help dissolve the salt. Ensure that the beaker is cool enough to handle before filtering.

4. Now set up the filter funnel and filter paper. The paper is circular; fold it to form a semicircle and again to form a quarter circle. This has four layers; open it to form a cone so that there are three layers on one side and one on the other. It will now fit in the funnel.

5. Place the folded filter paper into the funnel and put the conical flask under the funnel. Carefully pour the mixture through the funnel, ensuring that the mixture does not overflow from the top of the filter paper (it might take some time for all of the mixture to filter through).

6. When all of the mixture is filtered, transfer all of the filtrate into the evaporating basin.

7. Now put the evaporating basin onto a tripod and gauze. Heat it and watch what happens (you will need eye protection since evaporating to dryness can cause lots of spitting – see Safety note). Heat until most of the water has evaporated and a white sludge is left; stop heating and, when it is cool enough to handle, transfer to a safe, warm and dry place for a day or two to dry completely.

8. Remove some of the solid and examine it, using a hand lens. Use the box below to record what you see.

9. Remove as much of the solid as possible and weigh it. Record the mass and calculate the yield.

10. Use a hand lens to analyse the crystals.

Results

1. In the box, draw a few examples of the crystals you see with the hand lens.

2. Record the mass readings below and use these to calculate the yield.

   mass of rock salt at start of experiment = ……………… g

   mass of pure salt obtained at the end of the experiment = ……………… g

   $$\text{yield} = \frac{\text{mass of product}}{\text{mass of raw material}} \times 100 = ……………… \times 100 = ………………\%$$

Analyse results

1. What percentage yield did you get? ……………………………………………………………………

2. Why is this less than 100%?

   ……

3. How does it compare with the yield that other groups in the class obtained?

   ……

   ……

Check your understanding

1. Why was it necessary to grind up the rock salt first?

   ....[2 marks]

2. **a.** What did the filtration remove? ....[1 mark]

   b. What did the filtration not remove? ....[1 mark]

3. What did the evaporation remove? ....[1 mark]

Spot the mistake

1. Zena's group did not grind the rock salt finely. Why did this reduce their yield?

   .... [1 mark]

2. Kareem's group overfilled the filter funnel and the mixture flowed over the top of the filter paper (but not the funnel). What problem could this have caused?

   .... [1 mark]

Apply your understanding

1. The crystals obtained in the experiment are sodium chloride, also known as cooking salt or common salt. Emile wants to put the crystals from his experiment on his chips. Why is this not a good idea?

   ....[2 marks]

2. Michelle's group used hand lenses to examine the solid waste they had removed by filtration. Rock salt is spread onto roads in icy weather. 'There's a whole load of grit in this,' Michelle says. 'This won't melt ice!' What useful function does the grit in rock salt perform on slippery roads?

   ....[2 marks]

Evaluate your learning

1. In this experiment, you had to use a range of equipment and follow a multi-stage procedure. How well do you think you did this?

   ....

   ....

2. Suggest why your yield was different to that of other groups.

   ....

   ....

   ....

Mini vocabulary warm up

Look at these words: **acid   alkali   neutralisation   pH scale   base   indicator**

Which of these:

1. refers to a solution with a pH of less than 7? .... [1 mark]

2. refers to a base that dissolves in water? .... [1 mark]

3. occurs when an acid and an alkali react to form a solution with a pH of 7? .... [1 mark]

4. is something that shows the pH value of a solution? .... [1 mark]

5. will neutralise an acid? .... [1 mark]

6. gives a numerical value for the acidity of a solution? .... [1 mark]

Each of the following statements is either **true** or **false** – choose the correct response.

7. No acid is safe to eat or drink. **True / False**   [1 mark]

8. Hydrochloric, sulfuric and nitric acids all have a pH of less than 7. **True / False**   [1 mark]

9. If something has a pH of 7 it must be pure water. **True / False**   [1 mark]

10. Acids are more dangerous than alkalis. **True / False**   [1 mark]

11. To neutralise an acid, you need an equal volume of an alkali. **True / False**   [1 mark]

12. Zena is conducting an experiment that uses an indicator called litmus paper. There are two types –
    red and blue litmus paper. Red litmus paper turns blue in an alkali but stays red in an acid. Blue
    litmus paper turns pink in an acid but stays blue in alkali. As homework, Zena's teacher gives the
    class some of both types of litmus paper to take home and test various substances.

    a. Zena tests some orange juice. It turns blue litmus paper pink and does not affect red litmus
        paper. What conclusion should she draw?

        .... [1 mark]

    Zena makes a soap solution by adding soap to warm water and stirring it. She then tests it and
    finds that it turns red litmus blue but leaves blue litmus paper unchanged.

    b. Why did she dissolve the soap in water?

        .... [1 mark]

    c. What conclusion should she draw from testing the soap?

        ....[2 marks]

    d. Zena then decides to make a sugar solution and test that. She finds, however, that it does not
        change the colour of either red or blue litmus paper. What conclusion should she draw?

        ....[2 marks]

Purpose of practical activity

Scientists test materials in various ways and put them into groups or tables. One of these tests involves pH. Testing the pH enables us to group materials into acids and alkalis. The pH scale goes from 1 to 14, with 7 as the midpoint. Solutions with a pH less than 7 are acids and those with a pH of more than 7 are alkalis. Those with a pH of 7 are neutral – neither acid nor alkaline. A pH of just below 7 indicates a weak acid, whereas a pH of 1 or 2 indicates a strong acid. Similarly, a pH of just above 7 indicates a weak alkali, but one of 13 or 14 indicates a strong alkali. This investigation will introduce you to using universal indicator to test materials and classifying materials as acidic, alkaline or neutral.

Learning outcomes	Maths skills required
• Understand how solutions can be tested and classified according to their pH value. • Carry out tests with attention to detail and regard to safety.	• Relate a numerical scale to chemical properties.

Set up

Apparatus list	
• Variety of materials to be tested for pH – solutions with various pH values (acid, neutral and alkaline), and powders for dissolving. Include chemicals associated with food and hygiene, and others more commonly used as bench reagents. Suggestions include: HCl (dil); HNO_3 (dil); H_2SO_4 (dil); carbonic acid; ethanoic acid; NaOH (aq); NaCl (aq); aluminium sulfate; vinegar; cola drink; lemon juice; water; crushed dishwasher tablets; and washing powder.	• Beakers – the chemicals should be in labelled beakers distributed around the room. • Universal indicator solution or paper • pH charts • Test tubes • Eye protection • Pipettes • Test-tube racks

Safety notes
• *Always be careful when handling chemicals and follow your teacher's safety advice (see CLEAPSS guidance).*   • *Wear eye protection during the practical activity and until everyone has finished clearing up.*   • *Avoid skin contact with all of the chemicals and do not taste any you might normally drink.*   • *Tell your teacher if you spill anything before you try to clean it up.*

Common mistakes and how to avoid them
• It is important to avoid cross-contamination between different chemicals by ensuring that the test tubes used for one pH test are clean before starting another test.

Method

Read these instructions carefully before you start work.

1. Set up a test-tube rack with a set of clean test tubes.

2. Using the pipette, add one of the solutions to one of the test tubes to a depth of around 2 cm. Make sure you know the name of the chemical; enter it in the results table.

3. Either add a few drops of universal indicator solution or place a small piece of universal indicator paper in the solution. Note the colour that appears and record this in the table.

4. Now look at the pH chart and use the colour to identify the pH value of the solution. Record this.

5. Complete the final column of the table by interpreting the pH value and classifying whether, for example, the solution is a weak acid or alkali.

6. Repeat with each of the other solutions, cleaning any test tubes before reusing them.

7. There may be some other chemicals in powder form for you to test. Make these up into solutions and test them.

Results

Chemical	Colour in universal indicator	pH value	Meaning of pH value

You should now be able to order your results according to pH value. Enter the names of the chemicals in the table below (you'll need to turn the book sideways) according to their pH value.

1	2	3	4	5	6	7	8	9	10	11	12	13	14

Analyse results

1. Some of the chemicals for testing are foods or cleaning agents. What were their pH values?

....

2. Some of the other chemicals are used in the laboratory. What were their pH values?

....

3. Some of the materials were dry powders. Why were they mixed with water before testing?

....

4. Do you think it matters how much water was used to mix the powders? How could you find out?

....

....

5. Does the quantity of chemical tested affect its pH value?

....

....

Check your understanding

1. Some of the chemicals you tested might be skin irritants.

   a. What should you do if some splashes on the back of your hand?

   ....

   ....[2 marks]

   b. How would this help?

   .... [1 mark]

2. Is it true to say that the lower the pH the more dangerous the chemical? Explain.

   .... [1 mark]

Spot the mistake

1. Michelle says, 'As we've used up all the universal indicator paper and still have chemicals to test, let's just reuse the universal indicator paper from the other tests.' Why is this a mistake?

   .... [1 mark]

2. Will says, 'After testing the chemicals, I'm going to mix them all together.' Why is this a bad idea?

   .... [1 mark]

3. Emile's group were discussing the best way of dealing with spillages. They decide that a good way of dealing with a strong acid splashed onto skin is to add a strong alkali. Why is this not a good idea?

   ....

   .... [1 mark]

Apply your understanding

1. Kursad is visiting his aunt who is a keen gardener. She is digging powder into the flower beds. Kursad asks, 'What are you doing and why?' His aunt replies, 'I'm adding lime because the soil is too acidic. I love hydrangeas. If the soil is acidic they produce blue flowers. I want some pink ones!'

   a. Will the lime raise or lower the pH of the soil? ....[1 mark]

   b. How could Kursad test the soil to see if his aunt added the right amount of lime?

   .... [1 mark]

   c. Are the hydrangeas working as an indicator? .... [1 mark]

2. A bee sting is acidic and a wasp sting is alkaline.

   a. What common household substance could you put on a bee sting to neutralise it?

   .... [1 mark]

   b. What common household substance could you put on a wasp sting to neutralise it?

   .... [1 mark]

3. Gina has indigestion. Her mother says, 'You need to take some antacid.' Gina has studied acids and alkalis in class and she also knows that her stomach produces acid to break down food.

   If the function of an antacid is to deal with excess stomach acid, what do you think it might be and how do you think it got its name?

   ....

   ....[2 marks]

Evaluate your learning

1. How well do you think that your group was able to follow instructions and test each of the chemicals accurately?

   ....

   ....

   ....

2. How well do you think that you are able to apply the idea of a pH scale to various situations?

   ....

   ....

   ....

Mini vocabulary warm up

Look at these words:

plastic   metal   wood   crumpled paper

Which of these:

1. would be a good material to wrap around chips to keep them hot? ……………….............. [1 mark]

2. is good at enabling hot water to transfer energy to cooler surroundings? …………………. [1 mark]

Choose the correct response:

3. A **conductor / insulator** enables energy to be transferred easily.   [1 mark]

4. A **conductor / insulator** does not enable energy to be transferred easily.   [1 mark]

Each of the following statements is either **true or false** – choose the correct response.

5. Styrofoam containers keep hot food hot because the material is a good insulator.
    True / False   [1 mark]

6. If you touch a hot radiator, heat is transferred to your body. **True / False**   [1 mark]

7. Wearing a coat on a cold day transfers heat into your body. **True / False**   [1 mark]

8. Opening a refrigerator on a warm day causes cold energy to come out. **True / False**   [1 mark]

9. Two blocks have been in a room for some time. One is made of metal and the other is made of wood. The metal one feels colder because it is at a lower temperature. **True / False**   [1 mark]

10. Michelle's friends are coming round for tea. On the way home from school, they stop to buy a box of ice cream. They still have a 20-minute walk to reach her house.

Michelle: Let's wrap the box of ice cream in my scarf to stop it melting. That will keep it cold.	Kareem: No – that's not a good idea. Scarves warm things up and it will make the ice cream melt quicker.	Juanita: The scarf won't make any difference to how quickly the ice cream melts.

   a. Who do you think is right? ……………………………………….................................. [1 mark]

   b. Explain your reasoning.

       .... [1 mark]

   c. Suggest what happens to the reading on a thermometer if you wrap it up in a scarf.

       .... [1 mark]

   d. Explain your reasoning.

       .... [1 mark]

Purpose of practical activity

Thermal energy is essential. We need to keep warm as living organisms and we also want to control the temperature of other objects. For example, we want hot food to be piping hot, the water in a shower to be warm and the food in a freezer to be cold. We need to control the transfer of energy, which is not always easy. In this experiment you will investigate how to keep hot food hot and the best way of doing this.

Learning outcomes	Maths skills required
• To use scientific ideas to develop and test a hypothesis. • To design and run an experiment comparing the effectiveness of insulators. • To explain what the evidence suggests and compare it to the hypothesis.	• Gathering and recording data. • Carrying out calculations on data. • Analysing data to identify patterns.

Set up

Apparatus list
• Various types of hot food container, for example, fish-and-chip wrappers, expanded-polystyrene burger containers, thin rigid plastic takeway containers with lids, pizza boxes. • Thermometers • Stop clocks • Balances to weigh containers • Hot objects to keep hot such as wheat bags. A beaker of water can be used, but care should be taken not to spill the water or use water that is boiling hot. Note: for each experiment the same volume of water should be used.

Safety notes
• *Take care not to burn yourself.* • *Thermometers are fragile and, if they are broken, the glass will be very sharp.*

Common mistakes and how to avoid them
• When you are using a thermometer, remember that it will show the temperature of whatever the bulb or the sensor is in contact with. For example, if you are measuring the temperature of water in a beaker and lift the thermometer out, it will show the temperature of the air. • In this investigation, you will be comparing one insulation material with another, but you need to make sure that your comparison is fair. For example, comparing a 500 g expanded polystyrene container with 10 g of cotton wool will not enable you to decide which is the better insulator. • Remember to use scientific ideas when predicting the outcome – you need to explain why one material will be better than another.

Method

Read these instructions carefully before you start work.

1. Look at the different insulating containers and materials. Can you predict which material will be most effective at keeping a hot object hot? Suggest why one material might be better than another. As an example, some materials trap air – does this help?

2. Weigh your insulating materials. If possible use the same mass of each material. If this is not possible (for example, because one of the materials is a rigid container) then weigh that container and then use the same mass for the other materials.

3. Start the experiment by measuring the temperature of the hot object (the wheat bag, the beaker of water or whatever you are using) and then measure its temperature at regular intervals for a set period of time. Record these readings in a table.

4. After collecting your readings with no insulation, insulate your hot object, measure its temperature now and then measure its temperature at regular intervals for a set period of time. Record the readings in a table.

5. Repeat Step 4 with different insulation. Record the readings in a table.

Results

Think about how many columns you need. You will need a column for each of the materials you test – and don't forget one set of figures will come from using no insulation.

1. You will need to design a results table.

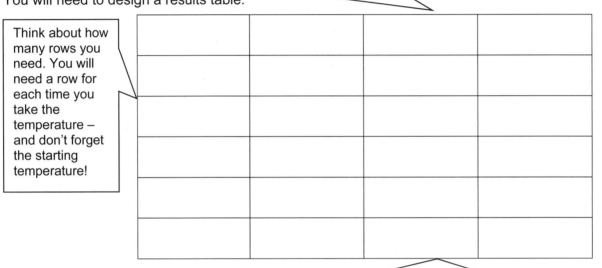

Think about how many rows you need. You will need a row for each time you take the temperature – and don't forget the starting temperature!

For example, if you were testing three different types of insulation and taking the temperature every 2 minutes for 10 minutes you would need four columns and six rows for your results, and don't forget the headings as well.

2. Plot each set of readings on a graph. Think about how to present your data clearly, for example, using a different colour or a different shape of point for each of the different types of insulation.

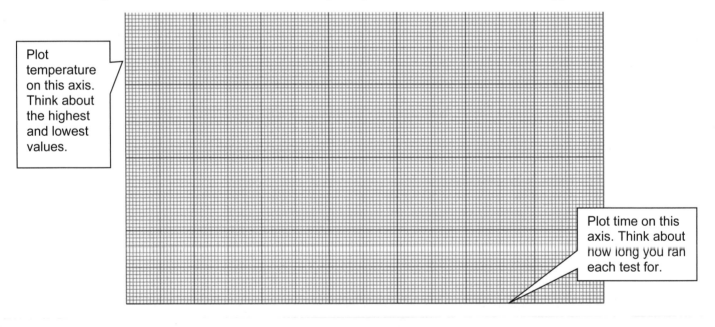

Plot temperature on this axis. Think about the highest and lowest values.

Plot time on this axis. Think about how long you ran each test for.

a. Each set of points needs a line of best fit. See how well you can draw this on the graph.

b. Label each line to show which material was being tested.

Analyse results

1. Look at the results from the experiment.

   a. Which materials were the best insulators and which were the worst?

   ....

   b. How does the graph show this?

   ....

   c. How does this compare with your hypothesis?

   ....

2. Will's group are heating up water and watching how the temperature rises. They are aiming to get the water to 60 °C before insulating it and letting it cool. They notice that the water seems to be going up about 4 degrees every minute.

   | Will: I bet it will continue going up at this rate – energy is being transferred into it at a steady rate. | Kareem: I think as it gets hotter it won't go up by as much each minute – energy will escape from the hot water faster when it gets hotter. | Emile: I think it will go up by more than 4 degrees per minute soon. Some of the energy at the start had to go into getting the beaker hot as well. |

   Use your equipment to take readings at regular intervals and complete the table below.

Time (min)										
Temp (°C)										

   Use the pattern in your results to decide who in Will's group is right and why.

   ....

   ....

Check your understanding

1. Why was it important to use the same mass of material in each experiment?

   ....

   ....[2 marks]

2. Kursad says, 'The gradient of the line shows how good each material was – a gentler gradient means that it was a better insulator.' Explain why he is right.

   ....

   .... [1 mark]

3. When an object is cooling down, energy is transferred from one store to another. Name the store it is moved from and the store it is moved to.

.... [1 mark]

Spot the mistake

1. Emile says, 'Since an object is cooling down all the time, you don't need to wait minutes between each reading. You can take readings every 5 seconds and stop the experiment after 30 seconds.' Explain why he is wrong.

.... [1 mark]

2. Gina says, 'It didn't matter whether all the experiments started off with the hot object at the same temperature because they would all cool down anyway.' Explain what is wrong with her reasoning.

....

....[2 marks]

Apply your understanding

1. Mr Akhbar is opening a fast-food take-away. He wants to use food containers that keep food hot.

   a. How can he use the results from your experiment to choose the best food container?

   .... [1 mark]

   b. Suggest how your experiment might not help him decide on a good food container to use.

   ....[2 marks]

2. Zena says, 'A material that will keep hot objects hot will also keep cold objects cold.' Will says, 'That's wrong – hot and cold are opposites, so it can't be the same material.' Use ideas about energy transfer to explain who is right.

   ....[2 marks]

Evaluate your learning

1. In this experiment, you needed to compare the materials in a fair way. How did you achieve this?

   ....

   ....

2. You also set up the graph so you could compare the performances of the different materials. How did you do this successfully?

   ....

   ....

   ....

Mini vocabulary warm up

Look at these words:

ohms   volts   joules   amps   watts   voltage

Which of these:

1. are the units that are used to measure voltage? ……………………………………….. [1 mark]

2. are the units that are used to measure current?... [1 mark]

3. is sometimes referred to as potential difference?... [1 mark]

The wires used to connect components in a circuit are made of copper, covered with plastic. Underline the correct words to complete these sentences.

4. Copper is a good **conductor / insulator** and has **low / high** resistance. [2 marks]

5. Plastic is a good **conductor / insulator** and has **low / high** resistance. [2 marks]

Each of the following statements is either **true** or **false** – choose the correct response.

6. Batteries each have a positive and a negative terminal. **True / False** [1 mark]

7. If you are using two batteries in series to provide greater voltage, you should connect the positive terminal on one to the positive terminal on the other. **True / False** [1 mark]

8. There has to be a complete circuit for current to flow. **True / False** [1 mark]

9. There has to be a switch in a circuit or it will not work. **True / False** [1 mark]

10. Increasing the number of bulbs connected in series in a circuit increases the total resistance.
True / False [1 mark]

11. Increasing the voltage supply to a circuit will affect the current flowing in it. **True / False** [1 mark]

12. Meters are used to measure voltage and current.

   a. An ammeter has to be connected in series with components to measure the flow of current through them. Draw a circuit showing a bulb powered by a battery and an ammeter measuring the current flowing through it. [1 mark]

   b. A voltmeter has to be connected in parallel with components to measure the voltage across them. Draw a circuit showing a bulb powered by a battery and a voltmeter measuring the voltage across it. [1 mark]

Purpose of practical activity

Electrical circuits are widely used in all sorts of applications. It is important to understand what is meant by voltage and current, and how these are linked in a circuit. In this experiment you will build and test a circuit, taking measurements of both the voltage and the current. You will need to take readings as accurately as possible, analyse the results and see if there is a pattern.

Learning outcomes	Maths skills required	Formulae
• Set up a circuit based on a diagram, using components and wires. • Use the circuit to produce data showing voltage and current. • Analyse the data to come to a conclusion about the relationship between voltage and current.	• Take readings from meters and record them accurately. • Perform calculations on data. • Identify patterns or trends in data.	resistance = $\dfrac{\text{voltage}}{\text{current}}$

Set up

Apparatus list
• D.C. ammeters (up to 1 A) • Insulated connecting leads • D.C. voltmeters (up to 5 V) • Crocodile clips (at least four per group) • 1 ohm fixed resistors • Rheostats (variable resistors) (up to 10 ohms and 1 A) • Variable power supplies D.C. up to 6 V

Safety notes
• *Switch off the circuit after taking each reading or the resistor may get hot enough to burn you.*

Common mistakes
• Make sure you follow the diagram carefully. Do not just connect everything in one continuous loop; the voltmeter goes in parallel and the ammeter in series. • Remember the correct units: voltage is measured in volts and current in amps. • If the circuit is left running, the current will heat up the components, especially the resistor. This will alter its resistance and the readings will be affected.

Method

Read these instructions carefully before you start work.

1. Set up the circuit as shown in the diagram.

2. Set the rheostat to a fixed position and leave it at that position.

3. Use the variable power supply to increase the voltage in equal steps.

4. Record the voltage across the fixed resistor and the current value, using readings from the voltmeter and ammeter, for each increase in the power supply.

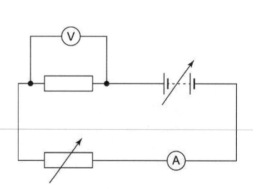

5. If there is time, alter the position of the rheostat and repeat the investigation to see what the effects are.

6. Calculate values of **voltage ÷ current** from your data and include them on the table.

Results

1. Draw a table of the results from your investigation.

Voltage									
Current									
Resistance (voltage ÷ current)									

2. Draw an appropriate graph of your data.

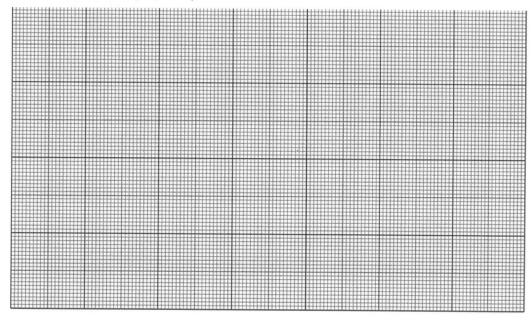

Analyse results

1. Looking at your voltage ÷ current calculations in the table, what can you conclude? How do you explain this?

    ....

    ....

2. If you adjusted the rheostat to a new position and repeated your investigation, how did this affect the values for voltage ÷ current?

    ....

    ....

3. What are the sources of error in this experiment?

    ....

    ....

Check your understanding

1. When you increased the voltage, what happened to the amount of current flowing in the circuit?

   .... [1 mark]

2. Look at the values of voltage and current – is there a pattern or trend?

   .... [1 mark]

3. What did you keep constant when you were altering the voltage?

   .... [1 mark]

4. If you increased the resistance but kept the voltage the same, how does this affect the current?

   .... [1 mark]

Spot the mistake

1. Look at these circuits. In each case, choose the correct response to suggest if the circuit would produce useful data.

   a. Yes / No   **b. Yes / No**   **c. Yes / No**

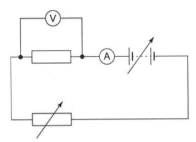
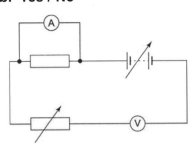
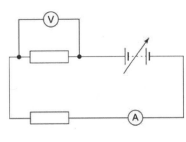

   [1 mark]   [1 mark]   [1 mark]

Apply your understanding

1. Kareem is making a torch in Design Technology. He installs a dimmer switch to control the brightness of the bulb. He turns the control and dims the bulb.

   a. What has he done to the amount of current flowing in the circuit? .... [1 mark]

   b. What has he done to the total resistance in the circuit? .... [1 mark]

Evaluate your learning

1. One of the outcomes from this activity was constructing a circuit from a diagram. What is a good way of doing this successfully?

   ....

2. After analysing the data, you drew a conclusion. How do you know that your conclusion was valid?

   ....

Mini vocabulary warm up

Look at these words:

mass   volume   weight   density   force   upthrust

Which of these words   (Note: each word may be used more than once.)

1. is the amount of space an object takes up? ....[1 mark]

2. is the force pulling an object towards the centre of the Earth? .... [1 mark]

3. is the force on an object immersed in water caused by the water pushing up on it?

    .... [1 mark]

4. is the quantity found by dividing the mass of an object by the volume it occupies?

    .... [1 mark]

5. is the quantity that can be measured in grams per cubic centimetre (g/cm^3)?

    .... [1 mark]

6. must be equal and opposite if an object is floating (give **two** words)?

    ....[2 marks]

7. are measured in newtons, N (give **three** words)?

    ....[3 marks]

8. There are different ways of finding out the volume of a solid object. If the object has a regular shape, a formula can be used to find its volume. For example, the volume of a cuboid is found by multiplying the length by the breadth by the height.

    a. What is the volume of a piece of wood 2 cm long, 3 cm wide and 3 cm tall?............ [2 marks]

    b. What is the volume of a shoe box 20 cm tall, 30 cm wide and 40 cm long?............... [2 marks]

Each of the following statements is either **true or false** – choose the correct response.

9. A ship is floating in the sea.

    a. The ship is floating so it has no weight. **True / False**   [1 mark]

    b. The upthrust must be greater than the ship's weight for it to float. **True / False**   [1 mark]

    c. For the ship to float the upthrust must be equal to its weight. **True / False**   [1 mark]

10. In an experiment, various solid objects are placed into water. Some float and some sink.

    a. A stone sinks when placed in water because there is no upthrust on it. **True / False**   [1 mark]

    b. A piece of softwood floats in water because it is weightless in water. **True / False**   [1 mark]

    c. The stone is denser than the piece of softwood. **True / False**   [1 mark]

Purpose of practical activity

Density is an important concept – it is a measurement that compares the amount of mass that an object has to its volume. This means that we can compare different materials in terms of how dense they are. Density indicates whether a solid will float or sink. To find the density of a material we need to know its mass and its volume. This experiment will enable you to see how this is done and relate it to whether the material floats or sinks.

Learning outcomes	Maths skills required	Formulae
<ul><li>To understand how the volumes of regular and irregular objects can be determined.</li><li>To calculate density and relate this to whether a material floats or sinks in water.</li><li>To understand how density can explain buoyancy.</li></ul>	<ul><li>Take and record readings.</li><li>Perform mathematical operations, including multiplication and division.</li><li>Analyse data, spotting trends and patterns.</li><li>Finding volumes of cuboids.</li></ul>	$$density = \frac{mass}{volume}$$

Set up

Apparatus list		
<ul><li>Various solid objects made of different materials; some should float in water and some should not. There should also be a variety of regular and irregular shapes.</li></ul>	<ul><li>Rulers</li><li>Displacement cans or beakers and measuring cylinders</li></ul>	<ul><li>Electronic balances</li><li>Cotton thread or string or fishing line</li></ul>

Safety notes
<ul><li>*Do not handle any mains electric sockets, switches or plugs with wet hands.*</li><li>*Wipe up any water spilt on the floor to avoid slipping and falling.*</li></ul>

Common mistakes and how to avoid them
<ul><li>Remember that density is calculated from mass divided by volume – not the other way around.</li><li>When lowering an irregular object into water to find its volume, take care to capture every drop of water that overflows.</li><li>We are working with values of density in g/cm^3, so the mass has to be in grams and the volume in cm^3.</li></ul>

Method

Read these instructions carefully before you start work.

1. Sort out the objects you are going to be using in your investigation. Separate them into regular and irregular objects. Make sure you have at least one of each.

2. For each object, use the balance to determine its mass and record this in the table.

3. If the object has a regular shape, use the correct formula to find the volume. For example, if it is a cuboid, volume will be length times width times height. Record this data in the table.

4. If the object has an irregular shape, use the displacement method to find the volume. Fill a beaker with water so it is absolutely full (if you have a displacement can, then use this). Tie the object on a cotton thread, string or line and carefully lower it into the water until it is completely immersed, catching all of the water that overflows. Measure the volume of the water that has overflowed – this will be the same as the volume of the object. Record this data in the table.

5. For each object, divide the mass by the volume to find the density and record this in the table.

6. Now find out if each object floats or sinks in water and record this in the table.

Results

Object	Mass (g)	Dimensions (note: only use these columns for regular objects)			Volume (cm^3)	Density (g/cm^3)	Float or sink?
		Length (cm)	Width (cm)	Height (cm)			

Analyse results

1. Look at the results table. How does the density of each object relate to whether it floats or sinks? Write a sentence to explain how these factors are related.

    .... [1 mark]

2. Liquids and gases also have density. Suggest how, using the formula **density = mass / volume**, you could determine the density of water.

    ....

    ....[3 marks]

3. Find the density of water using your method from Question 2 and record this in your table. Compare this with the results for each object. What do you find?

    ....

    ....[2 marks]

4. Look at the results table for Question 1. What are the possible sources of error in this experiment?

    ....

    ....[2 marks]

Check your understanding

1. Paraffin wax has a density of 0.72 g/cm³. Explain why a lump of wax floats in water.

   .... [1 mark]

2. Concrete has a density of 2.37 g/cm³. Does it float or sink in water? Explain why.

   .... [1 mark]

3. An ice cube floats in water but most of the mass is under the surface. What does this suggest about the density of ice?

   .... [1 mark]

4. Objects that float have mass. If they float, what does this show about the upthrust of the water compared with their weight?

   .... [1 mark]

Spot the mistake

1. Emile is finding the density of a piece of oak. The mass is 14 g and the volume is 20 cm³. His answer is 1.43 g/cm³. What mistake has he made?

   .... [1 mark]

2. Michelle is trying to find the volume of an irregular piece of cork. She fills a beaker full of water and lowers the cork carefully onto the top of the water, where it floats. She catches the water that overflows and measures its volume as 4 cm³. What mistake has she made?

   ....

   ....[2 marks]

3. Kareem is investigating density in an experiment. In his conclusion, he writes, *Any solid with a density of less than 1 g/cm³ will float in any liquid*. What mistake has he made?

   ....

   ....[2 marks]

Apply your understanding

1. Thousands of years ago, a Greek called Archimedes had a problem to solve. The King suspected that a crown was not pure gold. Archimedes knew that every metal has a different density. If he found the density of the crown, he would know whether it was pure gold. To find the density he needed to know the volume, but a crown is a complicated shape. The story goes that, after getting in a bath, he realised how to find the density of the crown. Suggest how he did it.

   ....

   ....[3 marks]

2. Gina's group are trying to explain why boats made out of steel float. They tested steel in their experiment and found that it sank.

Gina: It's to do with size. You wouldn't make a small boat out of steel but if it's bigger it's more buoyant.

Will: A steel boat isn't solid – it's hollow so most of it is air. That's why it floats.

Juanita: It's a different kind of steel they use to make boats. The piece we had was rectangular and solid so of course it wouldn't float.

Who do you think is correct and why?

....

....[2 marks]

3. Kareem's class is investigating forces and floating, as shown in the diagram. The block is made of iron. The forcemeter is showing a reading of 3.5 N and the balance is showing a reading of 320 g (equivalent to a force of 3.2 N).

   a. Why is the forcemeter showing a reading?

   .... [1 mark]

   b. Why is the balance showing a reading?

   .... [1 mark]

The block is now lowered into the water so that it is half submerged.

For each question, circle the correct response

   c. Will the reading on the forcemeter have

   increased / decreased / stayed the same? [1 mark]

   d. Will the reading on the balance have

   increased / decreased / stayed the same? [1 mark]

Next, the block is completely submerged.

   e. Will the reading on the forcemeter have

   increased / decreased / stayed the same? [1 mark]

   f. Will the reading on the balance have

   increased / decreased / stayed the same? [1 mark]

forcemeter (newtonmeter)

block

water

balance

888.88 g

Evaluate your learning

1. To complete this experiment you followed a sequence of steps. How did you do this successfully?

....

2. You also compared the densities of different materials with that of water to draw a conclusion. How did you make a good job of this?

....

....

Mini vocabulary warm up

Look at these words:

force   distance   moment   lever   clockwise   newton metre

Which of these:

1. refers to multiplying a turning force by the distance from the pivot? ....[1 mark]

2. means rotation in the same direction as the hands of a clock? ....[1 mark]

3. is the unit that moments are measured in? ....[1 mark]

4. is a simple machine that turns a small force into a larger force? ....[1 mark]

5. A crowbar is an example of a lever that can be used to pull a nail out of a piece of wood.

    On the diagram, clearly mark where:

    a. the person is applying a force to the crowbar   [1 mark]

    b. the crowbar is applying a force to the nail   [1 mark]

    c. the pivot is.   [1 mark]

    d. Compare the distance from the hand to the pivot to
        the distance from the nail to the pivot.

    .... [1 mark]

6. A seesaw is an example of equipment that uses moments.

    Josh and Nathan are playing on a seesaw. Josh is on the left. He
    weighs 180 N and his seat is 1.2 m from the pivot in the centre.

    a. Is Josh's moment clockwise or anticlockwise?

    ....   [1 mark]

    b. Calculate the size of the moment Josh is applying.

    ....[3 marks]

    Nathan is on the right. He weighs 200 N and his seat is 1.2 m from the pivot in the centre.

    c. Is Nathan's moment clockwise or anticlockwise? .... [1 mark]

    d. Calculate the size of the moment Nathan is applying.

    ....[3 marks]

    e. Why is the seesaw touching the ground on the right-hand side?

    .... [1 mark]

    f. Who needs to sit closer to the pivot to make the seesaw balance? ....[1 mark]

Purpose of practical activity

There are many situations in everyday life where turning forces, or moments, are used. For example, door handles, taps, pedal bins and some tools are levers. Using a screwdriver to lever open the lid on a tin of paint requires a turning force. Sometimes, such as in the example of the children's seesaw, there is more than one moment and so we need to combine these moments.

Learning outcomes	Maths skills required	Formulae
• To calculate the turning effect of a force. • To combine moments in the same system. • To apply the concept of moments to various situations.	• Take and record measurements. • Use measurements to calculate moments. • Combine moments in the same system.	• moment (Nm) = force (N) × distance (m) • 1 kg mass has a weight of 10 N

Set up

Apparatus list
• Metre rules • Slotted masses • Calculators • Modelling clay (optional)   • Pivots (can also use metre rule with hole drilled through centre, in which case pivot is a rod, such as a knitting needle, fixed horizontally using stand, boss and clamp; in this case there will also need to be string loops so that masses can be hung on rule).

Safety notes
• *Arrange the pivot and metre rule at a low height above the bench so that if the rule falls, or the weights fall off, they won't land on your hands or feet.*

Common mistakes and how to avoid them
• Watch the units: moments are measured in newton metres, so the force has to be in newtons (N) and the distance in metres (m). • If you are using slotted masses, these will be marked in grams. For example, 100 g has a weight of 1 N and 10 g has a weight of 0.1 N. • If you are reading distances off the metre rule, these will be in centimetres. There are 100 cm to 1 m, so 1 cm is 0.01 m. • Remember that you are measuring from the pivot, not from the end of the ruler. For example, if using a metre rule then a weight at the 15 cm mark is 35 cm (0.35 m) from the midpoint and a weight at the 75 cm mark is 25 cm (0.25 m) from the midpoint.

Method

Read these instructions carefully before you start work.

1. Set the metre rule up so that it is supported by the pivot at the midpoint. Note: it is very difficult to balance the rule with no weights on it, so no need to spend time on this – as long as it is near the midpoint it will work well. You could use small pieces of modelling clay to help stabilise the pivot. Alternatively, you could use a metre rule with a centre hole, clamp stand and slotted masses with hooks. For this experiment, your metre rule is your 'beam'.

2. Decide which end of the rule is going to be your left-hand side (LHS) and which is going to be your right-hand side (RHS).

3. Place two slotted 100 g masses 30 cm from the midpoint on the LHS and two 100g masses 30 cm from the midpoint on the RHS. With a bit of manipuation the rule should balance, Again, as long as it is close to balancing that will be fine. Complete the first row on the table, entering the moments.

    Place one slotted 100 g mass 30 cm from the midpoint on the LHS and two 100 g masses 15 cm from the midpoint on the RHS. It should balance. Complete the second row on the table, entering the moments.

4. Note that, for the two rows you have completed, the moments on the LHS and RHS are the same. The first row is the anticlockwise moment and the second row is the clockwise moment. If they are equal and opposite, the beam will balance.

5. Look at the third row of the table. This tells you what to set up on the LHS but only which masses to use on the RHS, not where they go. Experiment with this by sliding the masses on the RHS along the rule until the beam balances and record the distance from the midpoint. Now work out the moment – it should be the same on the RHS as on the LHS.

6. Now try the fourth row. Again, it tells you what to set up on the LHS but only which masses to use on the RHS, not where they go. Work out the moment on the LHS; the moment on the RHS will be the same. Knowing the weight and dividing it into the moment will give you the distance.

7. Now have a go at the other rows. In each case find out the moment on the LHS, and use that value for the moment on the RHS to work out the missing values.

Results

LHS					RHS				
Mass (g)	Weight (N)	Distance from pivot (cm)	Distance from pivot (m)	Moment (Nm)	Mass (g)	Weight (N)	Distance from pivot (cm)	Distance from pivot (m)	Moment (Nm)
200	2	30	0.3		200	2	30	0.3	
100	1	30	0.3		200	2	15	0.15	
200	2	20	0.2		100	1			
200		30			300				
100		40					10		
300		20			400				

Analyse results

1. What needs to be true about moments for a pivoted beam with weights to balance?

    .... [1 mark]

2. What needs to be true about the distances between the weights and pivot when balancing a larger weight with a smaller weight on a pivoted beam?

.... [1 mark]

Check your understanding

1. What two things do you need to know to calculate the moment that a force is applying?

....

....[2 marks]

2. How do you know if a moment is clockwise or anticlockwise?

....

.... [1 mark]

3. What do you need to do with the measurements you take to be able to calculate the moment in newton metres?

....

....[2 marks]

Spot the mistake

1. Some students are using metre rules, weights and pivots to measure moments.

   a. Gina positions the weights on a metre rule so that one edge of the disk is against the marking on the rule. Why is this a mistake?

   ....

   .... [1 mark]

   b. Will stands the weights up on their edge on the rule. Why is this a mistake?

   ....

   .... [1 mark]

   c. Kursad measures the positions from the ends of the metre rule. Why is this a mistake?

   ....

   .... [1 mark]

Apply your understanding

1. Tap turners are devices to make it easier to turn a tap on or off. Use the concept of moments to explain how they work.

....

....[2 marks]

2. Use the concept of moments to explain how a pair of scissors works.

....

....[3 marks]

3. Mike's daughters are very keen for him to go on the seesaw with them. The seesaw is 6 m long and pivoted in the middle. Mike weighs 240 N, Annie weighs 120 N and Cathy weighs 180 N. Annie is sitting at one end of the seesaw and Cathy is sitting 2 m from the pivot.
   Where should Mike sit to balance the seesaw?

....

....[4 marks]

Evaluate your learning

1. What advice would you give to other students on how to do the moments experiment carefully and safely?

....

....

....

2. How good were you and your group at using moments to predict where to put a weight on one side of the rule to balance something on the other side?

....

....

....

Mini vocabulary warm up

Look at these words: **distance   time   speed   force   motion   acceleration**

Which of these:

1. is measured in metres per second (m/s)?...[1 mark]

2. is an indication of the speed increasing or decreasing? .... [1 mark]

3. could you use to calculate the speed of an object? .... and .... [2 marks]

4. Different objects move at very different speeds. Insert the letter relating to each of following objects in the table to match the object to its typical speed.   [6 marks]

   A person walking   **B** Usain Bolt sprinting   **C** Bullet fired from gun

   D car on motorway   **E** Formula 1 racing car   **F** Windspeed of a F5 tornado

Object						
Typical speed (m/s)	55	130	2.5	12	100	400

5. Michelle travels to school by walking to the bus stop, catching a bus and then walking to the school from the bus station.

   a. She lives 600 m from the bus stop, which is 4 minutes' walk. What is her speed in m/s?

   ....[2 marks]

   b. The bus journey is 4.8 km and takes 10 minutes. What is the speed of the bus in m/s?

   ....[3 marks]

   c. The final walk is 300 m and takes 3 minutes. Is she walking faster or slower than in part **a**?

   ....[3 marks]

   d. What is the total length of her journey? .... [1 mark]

   e. What is the total journey time? .... [1 mark]

   f. What is her average speed for the whole journey? .... [3 marks]

   g. The whole journey actually takes an average of 22 minutes. Suggest why this is greater than your answer to part **f**.

   .... [1 mark]

   h. Show the first part of her journey (the walk to the bus stop) on this graph. Think about how you should label the axes and what scale to use.   [2 marks]

Purpose of practical activity

When an object moves it is useful to be able to measure its speed, whether it's a jet aircraft or the hair growing on your head. We can show this motion in various ways too. Sometimes it is best to calculate a value, but sometimes it is more useful to display the movement on a graph. In this experiment you will measure the speed of an object and investigate how to represent this.

Learning outcomes	Maths skills required	Formulae
• Understand how to calculate speed by using data from an experiment. • Know how to represent motion on a distance–time graph. • Evaluate the quality of data and suggest its limitations.	• Gather and display data from an experiment. • Perform calculations on data. • Use a formula to calculate speed.	$speed = \dfrac{distance}{time}$

Set up

Apparatus list
• Ramps • Supports for end of ramp to alter the gradient • Weights, such as slotted masses   • Vehicles, such as dynamics trolleys • Timers, such as stop watches • Rulers and tape measures

Safety notes
• *Ramps and trolleys must be placed so that they cannot fall on to hands or feet.* • *Take extra care when gradients are steep and trolleys are moving faster.*

Common mistakes and how to avoid them
• Take care when using the formula – it is distance divided by time, not the other way around! • Make sure that the units are in the right form; for example, if speed is required in metres per second then distances need to be converted to metres and time has to be in seconds.

Method

Read these instructions carefully before you start work.

1. Set up the ramp so that the trolley rolls down it and along the floor. Make sure you have equipment to hand to measure both the distances travelled (on the ramp and on the floor) and the time taken for each part of the journey.

2. Let the trolley roll down the ramp and across the floor. Measure and record in the table:

    - the distance the trolley travels on the ramp

    - the time taken for the trolley to roll down the ramp

    - the distance the trolley travels across the floor

    - the time taken for the trolley to roll across the floor.

3. Calculate the average speeds for the trolley on the ramp and on the floor, and record these.

4. Consider how similar the figures would be if you repeated the experiment. Now repeat it twice more and see how the results agree.

5. Consider what might happen if you repeat the experiment with weights on the trolley. Attach weights and run the experiment again.

6. Repeat these readings and record them in the table.

7. If you have time, use different combinations of weights. Record your readings in the table.

Results

Weight added to trolley (N)	Distance trolley travelled on ramp (m)	Time taken for trolley to reach end of ramp (s)	Average speed of trolley on ramp (m/s)	Distance trolley travelled across the floor (m)	Time taken for trolley to travel across the floor (s)	Average speed of trolley travelling across the floor (m/s)

Analyse results

1. Looking at the results, how did adding weights to the trolley affect its speed?

   ....

2. Looking at the results from tests that were repeated, how well did they agree?

   ....

   ....

3. Suggest a way of dealing with sets of results where the agreement between them is poor.

   ....

   ....

Check your understanding

1. Why do the columns for speed say 'average speed' and not just 'speed'?

    ....

2. The accuracy of a set of results describes how close they are to the true value.

    a. How accurate do you feel your distance measurements were and why?

    ....

    ....

    b. How accurate do you feel your time measurements were and why?

    ....

    ....

3. Precision describes how close readings of the same thing are to each other. How precise do you think your readings were and why?

    ....

4. The repeatability of an experiment is an indication of how, if the same group of people using the same equipment did the same experiment, they would get the same, or very similar, results. Explain how good the repeatability of your results was.

    ....

    ....

5. The reproducibility of an experiment is an indication of how, if a different group of people using the same equipment did the same experiment, they would get the same, or very similar, results. Suggest how you might do this with your experiment. If different groups used more than one set of apparatus in your lesson, compare results and see how reproducible the experiment was.

    ....

    ....

Spot the mistake

1. Emile's group used a mark at the top of the ramp as the starting point and lined up the back of the trolley with this. They measured from this mark to the end of the ramp to find the distance the trolley travelled on the ramp. What mistake have they made?

    .... [1 mark]

2. Gina's group calculated that a trolley that travelled 1.54 m in 4.56 s had an average speed of 0.337719298 m/s. What mistake have they made?

    .... [1 mark]

3. Kareem's group reasoned that because their trolley travelled 74 cm in 12.2 s it had an average speed of 6.07 m/s. What mistake have they made?

.... [1 mark]

Apply your understanding

1. Kursad's group are calculating the speed of a trolley on a ramp. They carry out the experiment four times and obtain the values of 1.7 m/s, 1.6 m/s, 1.1 m/s and 1.7 m/s.

Kursad: One of the results, the third one, is clearly wrong. We should ignore that one and calculate the mean of the other three.

Zena: We should find the mean. Add them up and divide by 4.

Emile: Because one of the results is way out, we need to do the whole experiment again and get a new set of results.

What do you think they should do, and why?

....

....[2 marks]

2. Will says, 'The idea of the average speed of the trolley rolling down the ramp is pointless. When the trolley starts off, it is travelling more slowly and then at the end of the ramp it is travelling faster, so there's only one point in the whole journey when the average speed is correct.'
What do you think, and why?

....

.... [2]

Evaluate your learning

1. In this experiment you gathered a lot of data and repeated readings that were similar. How well did that go?

....

....

....

2. You also had to evaluate your results, using the concepts of precision and accuracy. How well did you manage to do that?

....

....

....

Mini vocabulary warm up

Look at these words:

frequency   wavelength   amplitude   speed   transverse   longitudinal

Which of these:

1. refers to the length of a complete wave? ....[1 mark]

2. is the height of a wave? ....[1 mark]

3. refers to how many waves pass a place in one second? .... [1 mark]

4. is measured in metres per second? .... [1 mark]

5. is measured in hertz (Hz)? ....[1 mark]

6. are measured in metres (m)? .... and ....….…… [2 marks]

7. Waves can be modelled by using a helical spring toy called a Slinky. Waves can move in two ways – longitudinal and transverse travel. Which type of wave is represented by a Slinky that is:

    a. being pushed in and out? .... [1 mark]

    b. being moved from side to side, or up and down? .... [1 mark]

8. On this wave diagram, clearly mark the points you would measure from and to, to determine:

    a. the amplitude   [1 mark]

    b. the wavelength.   [1 mark]

9. Sound travels as a wave.

    a. If the frequency of a sound wave increases, how does the sound differ?

    .... [1 mark]

    b. If the amplitude of a sound wave increases, how does the sound differ?

    .... [1 mark]

    c. Is it true that some aircraft can travel faster than the speed of sound? .... [1 mark]

Each of the following statements is either **true** or **false** – choose the correct response.

10. Light also travels as a wave.

    a. Light travels faster than sound in air. **True / False**   [1 mark]

    b. White light can be split into different colours. **True / False**   [1 mark]

    c. We can see objects because light travels from our eyes to them. **True / False**   [1 mark]

    d. The paler an object is, the better it is at absorbing light. **True / False**   [1 mark]

Purpose of practical activity

Many things travel as waves, including light, sound, TV and radio signals. Even earthquakes travel through the Earth as waves. Although these waves are very different from each other in some ways, they are very similar in others. We use the same terms, such as frequency and wavelength, to describe them and they behave similarly, such as being reflected by certain objects. This experiment will introduce you to examining, recording, measuring and carrying out calculations on waves.

Learning outcomes	Maths skills required	Formulae
• Use the key terms for parts of waves. • Explore how the speed of a wave can be determined.	• Extract data from images. • Perform calculations on data by using an equation.	$$speed = \frac{distance}{time}$$

Set up

Apparatus list
• Long lengths of rope (minimum of 3 m per group)   • Equipment to record (photo and video) and annotate images, such as a tablet with appropriate apps   • Timers   • G-clamps (if working inside)   • Reference lines to enable measurements to be taken. These could be metre rules or tape measures. However, the lines need to be clearly visible on the images so a good solution is to use a paper strip with bold black marks at 10 cm intervals. Decorators' masking tape is cheap, takes marker pen ink and is easily removed. A metre rule with a clamp stand can also be used.

Safety notes
• *Do not tie ropes to gas or water taps or door handles. Use a secure G-clamp in the laboratory or a fence or tree if outside.*   • *Take care for the safety of others and watch out for ropes that may trip you up.*   • *Depending on the size of the class, it may be advantageous to use the school hall.*

Common mistakes and how to avoid them
• Remember that amplitude is measured from the midpoint of the wave to *either* the top of a crest *or* the bottom of a trough.   • Remember that wavelength refers to one complete wave, not just one complete peak.   • Remember that wave speed is measured in metres per second, so distances have to be converted to metres before making any calculations.

Method

Read these instructions carefully before you start work.

1. Tie one end of the rope to an anchor point, such as a tree (see safety note above) or, if working in the school hall, students work in pairs with one student acting as the anchor by holding one end of the rope still. Stand across from the anchor point with the other end of the rope and move the end up and down to make waves. With a bit of practice it should be possible to get a series of waves travelling along the rope.

Alternatively, attach the end of the rope to the bottom of a table leg, lay the rope across the floor and move the other end from side to side. You should be able to get waves travelling across the surface of the floor. In either case, having a steady consistent wave is important.

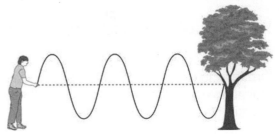

2. Set up a horizontal reference line marked on the floor or table top. It should be parallel with the rope. Also use a vertical one, which could be a metre rule held on a clamp stand.

Once there is a steady set of waves, take a photo. This will work better if the photographer is standing well back from the rope. It is important to get a clear picture showing at least one complete wave (preferably several, to make comparisons) and to ensure the reference lines are visible in the pictures.

3. The image should then be annotated to show:

   • the wavelength

   • the amplitude

   • the direction in which the wave is travelling.

4. Now take a short video clip of the rope making waves. Again, the reference lines need to be clearly visible in the video and the recording device should be held still.

Results

1. Analyse the photos and use them to complete this table. It is best to use several images of the same wave. Study the images and use the reference lines to produce data to record in the table.

	1st estimate	2nd estimate	3rd estimate	4th estimate	Agreed value
Wavelength (m)					
Amplitude (m)					

2. Now study the video recordings of the wave. Again, if there are several recordings, it is useful to pool the results.

The frequency of the wave is the number of complete waves passing a point in one second. A good way of analysing this is to pick a point in the frame and count how many complete waves pass that point in 10 seconds. Divide your answer by 10 and enter it in the table.

The speed of the wave is the distance travelled by one wave, divided by the time taken for it to travel that distance. Watch the video, select a wave to use, see how far it travels within the view (use the reference line) and time it. Divide the distance by the time to get the speed.

	1st estimate	2nd estimate	3rd estimate	4th estimate	Agreed value
Frequency (Hz)					
Speed (m/s)					

Analyse results

1. How well did the experiment work, in terms of you being able to find values for the amplitude, wavelength, frequency and speed of the waves?

   ....

   ....

2. Were the various results for each experiment close to one another or was there a lot of variation?

   ....

3. Thinking about your answer to Question 2, how confident are you about the accuracy of the results?

   ....

   ....

Check your understanding

1. When you measured the amplitude of the wave, which points did you measure from and to?

   .... [1 mark]

2. Why might this have been a source of error?

   ....

   .... [1 mark]

3. What are the advantages of working from images of waves?

   ....

   .... [1 mark]

4. What are the limitations of working from images of waves?

   ....

   .... [1 mark]

Spot the mistake

1. Zena's group wanted to obtain several images of the wave, so they all took turns at making the wave. Each time someone different made the wave, someone else took a photo of the wave. Why was this a mistake?

   ....

   .... [1 mark]

2. Kareem's group did not get the horizontal reference line in their photo so they used the vertical reference line to estimate the horizontal distances. Why might this have been a mistake?

....

.... [1 mark]

Apply your understanding

1. Emile's group are studying water waves. They have set up an experiment, using a fish tank that is half-full of water, and are using a paddle to make waves. Looking through the side of the tank, they can see the waves travelling along the surface of the water.

   They want to find values for the wavelength, amplitude, frequency and speed of the water waves. Suggest how they could modify the experiment you did in order to find these values.

   ....

   ....

   ....

   ....[4 marks]

2. Michelle's group are repeating the rope wave experiment because their initial results were not very good – their estimates of the values were very different to each other. What three pieces of advice would you give them to help them get a good set of results?

   ....

   ....

   ....[3 marks]

Evaluate your learning

1. This experiment involved a lot of work analysing images and estimating values. How well do you think you did this?

   ....

   ....

   ....

2. If you were able to do the experiment again, what would you do differently and why?

   ....

   ....

   ....

Glossary

Biology

Adaption	features that organisms have to help them survive in their environment
Carbohydrate	food group including starches and sugars
Cell	'building block' that all living things are made from
Chloroplast	structure in plant cells where light is absorbed so that photosynthesis can produce food
Control variable	factor kept constant in an investigation
Correlation	how well sets of data are linked; high correlation shows that there is a strong agreement between two sets of data
Dependent variable	variable that is measured in an investigation
Digestion	breakdown of food in order to obtain energy
Endocarp	innermost layer of the pericarp (see below)
Environmental factors	influences upon on organism arising from what surrounds it
Exchange	the swapping of one thing for another
Eyepiece lens	the lens in an optical instrument which is closest to the eye
Factors	one of the things that could affect something else
Foodstuff	a material suitable for eating
Gaseous	something which exists as a gas
Genetic	influenced by the genes in an organism
Hypothesis	an explanation you can test that includes reasoning based on scientific concepts
Independent variable	a variable in an experiment that affects the outcome
Inherited characteristics	a feature of characteristic that has been passed on genetically
Magnification	a measure of how many times bigger an image is than the object
Mean value	figure calculated by adding up all the values in a data set then dividing by the number of values
Median	the middle number in a set of values when they are arranged in order from lowest to highest
Membrane	layer around a cell that controls substances entering and leaving the cell
Microscope	optical device used to see magnified images of tiny objects and structures
Mode	the most frequently occurring number in a set of values
Nutrition	the study of how nutrients affect various aspects of the health of an organism, such as growth, health and disease.
Objective lens	the lens in an optical instrument which is closest to the object being studied
Organism	a living thing
Outlier	a data point that is significantly different from the others in a set and does not follow the pattern or trend
Ovary	organ in female animals that makes egg cells; and in plants that contains ovules
Pericarp	part of a fruit formed from the ovary wall
Photosynthesis	process carried out by green plants – sunlight, carbon dioxide and water are used to produce glucose and oxygen
Population	the number of a type of organism living in a particular area
Product	(of chemical reaction) substance made in a chemical reaction
Quadrat	a portable frame used to mark out a set area
Reactant	starting substance in a chemical reaction
Respiration	the process used by all organisms to release the energy they need from food
Sampling techniques	methods used to choose a small, representative number of individuals from a large population
Stomata	small holes in the surface of leaves which allow gases in and out of leaves
Survey	a systematic description or examination of something

Transect	line across an area used to guide the sampling of organisms
Variation	differences in characteristics between individuals of the same species and between species

Chemistry

Acid	a substance that has a pH lower than 7
Alkali	a soluble substance with a pH higher than 7
Base	a substance that neutralises an acid; a base that dissolves in water is called an alkali
Catalyst	a substance that speeds up a chemical reaction
Compound	atoms of elements combine to form compounds; these compounds have different properties from the elements they contain
Concentration	amount of something per unit volume – for example, sugar in water
Crystals	solid with the particles arranged in a very ordered way; it therefore has flat faces and sharp edges
Decomposition	breaking down into simpler materials
Evaporate	change from a liquid to a gas at the surface of the liquid – such as when water evaporates to form water vapour
Filter	material with microscopic holes used to remove insoluble solids from liquids
Impurities	chemicals that differ from the main substance of an object
Indicator	chemical that has a different colour in an alkali and in an acid, used to identify whether an unknown solution is acidic or alkaline
Insoluble	unable to dissolve
Mortar and pestle	a bowl and a heavy, blunt tool used to grind substances up
Neutralisation	a chemical reaction in which an acid and a base react with each other, resulting in a neutral solution, which is one that is neither acid nor alkaline
Ore	a rock from which metal is extracted
pH scale	measure of acidity/alkalinity, on a scale from 0 to 14
Product	(of chemical reaction) substance made in a chemical reaction
Rate	the number of times something happens in unit time, such as a second
Reactant	starting substance in a chemical reaction
Reactivity	the tendency of a substance to undergo a chemical reaction
Reaction	a process in which a substance or substances are changed; some reactions are physical and reversible and others are chemical and irreversible
Salt	type of chemical compound – common table salt is sodium chloride
Soluble	solid that can dissolve (usually in water)
Vapour	liquid that has evaporated
Yield	proportion of a material that can actually be extracted compared with the theoretical amount

Physics

Acceleration	the rate at which speed increases or decreases
Accuracy	how close data is to true values
Ammeter	instrument used to measure the current flowing in a circuit
Amplitude	maximum distance moved in a vibration, measured from the middle position
Amps	unit of measurement of current, symbol A
Conductor (electrical)	material that allows current to flow through it easily; has a low resistance
Conductor (thermal)	material that allows thermal energy to be transferred through it easily
Current	rate of flow of electric charge, measured in amperes (A)
Density	mass of a material per unit volume
Displacement	a chemical reaction in which one substance takes the place of another in a compound

Energy	something has energy if it has the ability to make something happen when that energy is transferred
Estimate	best guess of a quantity, based on scientific knowledge and observation
Force	a push, pull or turning effect, measured in newtons (N)
Frequency	number of events in unit time, for example, number of waves produced by a source in one second; unit hertz (Hz)
Hertz	unit of frequency, equal to one per second
Insulator (electrical)	material that does not allow current to flow easily; has a high resistance
Insulator (thermal)	a material that does not allow energy to pass through it quickly by the process of thermal conduction
Irregular (shape)	a shape that is asymmetrical
Lever	simple machine that uses the turning effect of a force about a pivot
Longitudinal	a wave in which the oscillation is parallel to the direction of energy transfer
Mass	the amount of matter (stuff) in an object, measured in kilograms (kg)
Moment	turning effect of a force, unit of measurement is the newton-metre (Nm)
Ohms	unit of measurement of electrical resistance, symbol Ω
Pivot	point about which something turns – also called a fulcrum
Precision	when repeated readings of the same measurement give similar values
Regular (shape)	a shape that is symmetrical, such as a cylinder or a cuboid
Repeatability	when repeat tests of an investigation made by the same experimenter give similar results
Reproducibility	when an investigation method is repeated exactly and the same results are obtained by a different experimenter
Resistance	(in electricity) property of an electrical component, making it difficult for charge to pass through; unit of measurement is the ohm (Ω)
Resistor	(in electricity) circuit component that opposes the 'push' provided by the voltage in a circuit
Speed	how fast something travels – how much distance is covered in unit time
Thermal energy	energy possessed by an object due to the movement of particles
Thermometer	device used to measure temperature
Transverse	a wave in which the oscillations are at right angles to the direction of energy transfer
Upthrust	upward force exerted on an object in water
Variation	range of characteristics across individuals of the same group
Voltage	measure of the size of 'push' that causes a current to flow around a circuit; it is the amount of energy shifted (from battery to charge, or from charge to component) per unit charge
Voltmeter	device used to measure the voltage across a component in an electric circuit
Volts	unit of measurement of voltage (potential difference)
Volume	measurement of amount of space a material takes up, unit cm^3 or m^3; also a measurement of how loud a sound is, unit decibel (dB)
Wavelength	distance along a wave from one point to the next corresponding point where the wave motion begins to repeat itself – for example, crest to crest
Weight	force of gravity acting on an object, measured in newtons (N)